Their Tails Kept Wagging

Pets Show Us How Hope, Forgiveness, and
Love Prevail

By: Stephen Birchard

Co-author: Fe Anam Avis

Published by eBookIt.com
http://www.eBookIt.com

ISBN-13: 978-1-4566-3892-4 (Paperback)
ISBN-13: 978-1-4566-3887-0 (Ebook)

This book is dedicated to Bruiser.
When you read his story, you'll understand why.

Acknowledgments

"You've always been fascinated with wound healing in animals, why don't you write a book about it?" A simple question from my friend and co-author Fe Anam Avis that led to this book. Little did we know what would come of it: a book more about our relationships with animals than the biology of wounds and how they heal. Ultimately, the two are intertwined, and what we discover is that healing involves both the body and the soul. Fe's idea allowed me to relive and tell stories of courageous animals who faced life-threatening disease. I can't thank him enough for suggesting the idea, brainstorming the concept, reviewing the rough draft, and adding his intelligence to the content.

Editor Diane Stockwell with The Editorial Department did more than suggest revisions and correct technical mistakes; she brought the manuscript back to life. After writing the rough draft and making some revisions, the book lost its momentum, and its author needed encouragement from an expert. Diane did just that. When severely ill animals take significant steps in their recovery, we say they are "turning the corner." Diane helped our book do that. Brian Klems, also an editor, reviewed a sample of the book and provided some outstanding ideas to improve the manuscript.

Many thanks to Bo Bennett and his team at eBookit.com for transforming my manuscript into a book. From formatting to publishing and marketing, his services were outstanding.

My small group of manuscript readers included Pat Davis, Ginney Abblett, and KC Jorgenson, my dedicated and talented veterinary technician at MedVet Toledo. Thanks to all of you for your reviews and suggestions. KC also was part of the medical team that spent countless hours nursing Maximus Quintus back to health. Her skilled management of Maximus's multiple anesthetic episodes was essential to his recovery.

A special thanks to the owners of Rip, Hershey, Josie, Billy Bob, Jack, and Maximus for allowing me to contact them, sometimes many years after their pet's medical ordeal, to complete the stories of their cherished companion. In some cases, their loved one had passed away, but they were still willing to reflect on their lives and give me an even clearer picture of their loving relationship with them.

Others that deserve thanks for their assistance were Bobbi Englebeck and Amy Zimmerman for their help with patient information.

All the doctors, veterinary technicians, and veterinary students who provided medical care for these animals were essential to their stories and to their recovery. The techs and students were the ones who kept the patients clean with bathing and grooming, did daily physical exams on them, obtained samples of various bodily fluids, fed them, petted them, and carried them outside for valuable time in the sunshine. I wish I could thank them all personally because their nursing care was invaluable.

To my advisor, colleague, and valued friend, Dr. Ron Bright, thank you for making me a surgeon. My surgical career, and thus this book, were made possible by you.

Finally, thank you to the primary surgeon on Jack and Maximus, loving owner of Bob, a trusted colleague and intimate friend, and the one who doled out hugs as Bruiser's chapter brought me to tears. Dr. Becky Ball, you helped me make decisions on an array of book details, allowed me to include you in the stories, and made me a part of your life. You are a fantastic doctor, mother, and wife. I am a lucky man.

Table of Contents

Preface

*"For life is a seamless web. It connects us
not merely with one another, but with all
that is sentient—with all that shares its
miracle of birth and feeling and death."*

—Abe Fortas*

I had repaired hundreds of diaphragmatic
hernias on dogs and cats, but I was nervous
about this one. It was a chronic hernia, present
for over a year, and we didn't know what had caused
it. The diaphragm is the thin sheet of muscle that
separates the belly from the chest cavity. It was torn,
allowing the liver, spleen, and intestines to slide out
of the abdomen and move into the chest, putting
pressure on the lungs. The patient, Little Orphan
Annie, was a skinny, scruffy, affectionate little cat.
Her owner found her in a parking lot when she was
just ten weeks old. She was frail, dehydrated, and
malnourished. He nursed her back to health and
decided to keep her as a member of his family. But
he noticed that her breathing had always been
abnormal, like she was fighting to get enough air, and
it was getting worse. Since there was no known
history of trauma, her veterinarian was concerned

---

* Acceptance speech as recipient of the 1965 Schweitzer
Award from the Animal Welfare Institute

that she could have pneumonia or possibly a congenital disability of her heart and lungs. Radiographs of Orphan Annie's chest showed the diaphragmatic hernia. Most of her intestines and liver had moved into her chest cavity, impinging on the lungs and making it hard for her to breathe. She needed an operation to fix the damage, but it would be tricky.

Her anesthesia began well; she was on a ventilator to help her breathe, receiving gas anesthesia, and her vital signs were stable. After opening her abdomen, we saw a large hole in the diaphragm and scar tissue between the lungs and the herniated organs. There were also adhesions between the pericardium—the thin sac surrounding the heart —and the liver. I released the scar tissue by cutting it with scissors, careful not to injure the delicate lungs and heart. All the organs trespassing in the chest had to be gently pulled back to where they belonged in the belly. All went fine until I manipulated the liver. It was mushy and discolored, purplish instead of the typical dark brown. When I carefully tried to pull it to its usual location, it started bleeding.

"Dr. Birchard, her blood pressure is dropping!" KC, the veterinary technician performing anesthesia, was visibly concerned. "Increase her intravenous fluid rate and give her a unit of cat blood," I said, trying to stay calm. She hurriedly set up the transfusion as I continued to coax the bleeding liver back home in the abdomen where it belonged. But the more I manipulated it, the faster it bled. The tension in the room was palpable. Annie could not afford to lose much blood; she was not in good health. If we didn't stop the bleeding, she would go into shock and die. Hemorrhage was coming from several different areas of the liver. All I could do was put pressure on it with surgical sponges and hope it would stop. I took a deep breath and tried to keep my composure.

After a few minutes which seemed like hours, the liver started looking better. My finger pressure, combined with Annie's blood clotting abilities, allowed the bleeding to slow down. Her blood pressure and other vital signs began to improve. I gingerly put the liver back where it belonged, praying that the bleeding would not start again, and repaired the hole in the diaphragm with stitches. I looked at the liver again, and the bleeding had stopped. Thank goodness for that. I closed the abdominal incision, and we moved her into the Intensive Care Unit, where she slowly recovered from the anesthesia.

I called Little Orphan Annie's owner and told him she had made it through the surgery and was stable for now, but she was not out of the woods yet. Complications after surgery like this are common and can be severe. Her chances of survival were no better than 50/50. We would monitor her carefully for the next twenty-four hours. I didn't sleep well that night.

Patients like Little Orphan Annie are the reason I became a veterinary surgeon. I felt called to help animals overcome injury or disease, even as a child. I have always loved animals and am fascinated by their ability to recover from many health problems. The normal physiology of the animal body is fantastic, but its ability to heal damaged parts is even more remarkable. In the face of debilitating injury or disease, the animal's body mobilizes its natural restorative processes to heal the wounds.

In some cases, the damage is too severe, and the animal, overwhelmed by the trauma, loses the battle for survival. But given expert medical assistance combined with an inherent will to survive, animals can defy the odds even while facing life-threatening illnesses. In my forty-four years as a veterinarian, I have been privileged to witness many patients successfully manage the treacherous journey back to health after developing a critical illness. This book is about them, how their fight for survival affected me, and how veterinarians become emotionally attached to patients like Little Orphan Annie.

Severe injury or illness can affect a dog, cat, or other pet in several ways. For example, they can be hit by a car, attacked by another animal, or burned in a house fire. They can fall victim to accidents, abuse, diseases of internal organs, or cancer. Each animal in this book had a different medical condition, but they all healed by the same process. I find this process wondrous in its complexity and beauty. Through research and clinical experience, we gradually decipher the complex puzzle that makes up the healing of the broken body. Like most things about the physiology of life, the more we know, the more beautiful it appears.

After the injury, the animal's entire physiologic network is called into action. Like a well-coordinated army of soldiers, healing cells mobilize to sustain a complicated series of steps aiming to bring the wounded or diseased part back to normal function.[1] Many of these cells have specific duties. They seem to recognize that they are, although essential in themselves, part of a more extensive process that works to return the body to normalcy. Some cells sacrifice themselves for the greater good; after performing their function, they die and let new cells continue the healing process. Like the batting order of a baseball team, the cellular line-up is pre-determined. Neutrophils and macrophages are the lead-off batters in the wound to destroy bacteria and clean up dead cells and debris. The macrophages can detect low oxygen levels in the damaged tissue and stimulate new blood vessels to form, which improves circulation to the tissues and enhances healing. The multi-talented macrophages also produce chemicals that call up the next batters to the plate—the fibroblasts. Fibroblasts are the carpenters that build the fibrous tissue (collagen) framework that provides structure and strength to the repaired tissue.

In skin wounds, granulation tissue—the orange-red granular-looking tissue comprised of fibroblasts, collagen, and tiny blood vessels called capillaries, fills the wound. This essential tissue develops within open skin defects and pulls the edges of the skin together to close the wound. Skin epithelial cells then multiply and migrate across the surface of the granulation tissue to provide coverage and protection of the underlying tissue. Like Little Orphan Annie's damaged liver, other tissues and organs in the body heal by a similar process. They can even regenerate normal cells to rebuild the injured organ back to its original size and function.

Even when the healing process appears complete outside, activity behind the scenes continues. The collagen framework remodels over months and years; it becomes more organized to increase its strength. It senses the stress and strain around it as the animal moves and lines up its fibers to best function under these stressors. The collagen transforms to mimic the tissue around it; for example, the collagen in a tendon becomes tendon, the collagen in a broken bone becomes bone.

Time and time again, I have watched animals like Annie perform this miracle. As a faculty member at The Ohio State University College of Veterinary Medicine and then as a staff surgeon in private practice, I treated thousands of animals with injuries and diseases and watched them fight the battle for survival. I have cared for animals that suffered massive injuries to their skin, bones, mouth, and internal organs. With medical treatments that support them, bodies can become whole again, and the animals go home to their loving families.

The most important lesson a doctor learns is their role in treating a patient. I have learned that my mission is to assist the body in overcoming injury or disease. We do not single-handedly conquer disease or repair the broken parts. We care for the animal in a way that allows it to heal itself. Research continually teaches us how the body works, and we learn what we can and cannot do to help it. We now know that some of the previously used wound management techniques were detrimental and slowed repair. For example, flushing traumatic skin wounds with hydrogen peroxide was a time-honored technique used by physicians and veterinarians. The foaming, bubbly action of the peroxide in the tissue was considered beneficial. We now know that hydrogen peroxide is very irritating and kills the tender cells repairing the damaged tissues.[2] Wounds are now flushed with a simple sterile salt solution called normal saline which supports cell physiology without causing damage. An understanding and respect for the body's power to repair itself allow us to do things that help, rather than hinder, the healing process.

The satisfaction of treating illness comes not only from seeing a patient relieved of its suffering but also from seeing owners and the attending doctor relieved of the emotional stress associated with their companion's illness. Little Orphan Annie recovered from surgery to repair her diaphragmatic hernia and injured liver. Her owner brought her back to see me nine months after her surgery. She had gained weight, her haircoat was thick and shiny, and she was breathing normally. She looked fantastic, her owner beamed with happiness, and so did I. The experience of successfully helping a suffering animal like her is more than a medical victory—it allows greater awareness of non-tangible factors that contributed to the outcome. We realize that there are forces at work beyond what we are doing medically, resulting from an intense connection between humans and animals. Annie's owner loved her dearly and would have done anything he could to help her. That was my mission as well. His devotion to her was just as important as the medical care we gave her. When we experience and celebrate these emotional and spiritual connections, we take an essential step in understanding our relationship with our animal companions.

Each patient in this book was unique in what they taught me about healing. The injury or disorder was so severe that permanent disability or even death seemed inevitable in every case. In some patients, the battle for survival was difficult to watch, and euthanasia was considered to end their suffering. But there was a spirit of survival in each animal, a sense that giving up was not an option. This positive spirit energized both the animal's owners and the caregivers, and the fight to survive carried on. By attempting to identify and discuss this emotional connection between an injured animal and its owners and doctors, we seek to find meaning in these incredible stories of healing. In each animal's medical journey, the bond strengthened between the pet and their owner and between the pet and their doctor.

The remarkable animals in this book each in their way challenged my abilities, changed my attitudes, and taught me valuable lessons. At times I felt them saying to me: "If you don't give up on me, I won't either." They changed my life as a doctor and person by witnessing the powerful energy of healing that flowed through them. As their bodies healed and grew stronger, my spirit did the same.[3]

This book is not just about the biology of recovery from illness or trauma; it explores recuperation that requires more than blood transfusions, antibiotics, and surgical instruments. The book is a testament to the human-animal bond and how it helped save these pets from life-threatening maladies. Bandages surrounded wounds; the animals were surrounded by love from both owners and medical caregivers.

The connection between humans and animals has historical perspectives. In nearly every spiritual tradition, animals are considered carriers of universal values and personal meaning.[4] Animals remind us of the interconnectedness of all living things that Abe

Fortas so beautifully elucidated.† Pets' recovery from injury or disease requires significant time and effort from the pet's owner after being released from the hospital. The owner becomes the pet's nurse and caregiver, changing their relationship and investing the owner even more deeply in the pet's life, strengthening their bond. The pet is no longer just a companion; they are a member of the family and a profound source of joy and comfort. After recovering from a severe injury or disease, the pet and owner now have a "history" together. Owners begin to see their pets as invaluable companions along their journey through life. They can help their owners deal with their pain, whether medical or emotional.

The relationship between owner and pet is a long-term commitment. Their bond gradually strengthens over the years they are together. They are with each other every day, sharing the home, mutual experiences, and supporting each other through good times and bad. The veterinarians' bond with the animal is more episodic, as they see the pet for brief periods when they need routine health care or treatment for common illnesses. But when disaster strikes, and the pet needs lifesaving care of a severe illness or injury, the doctor/patient bond becomes markedly stronger. The vet becomes the animal's

---

† Acceptance speech when he received the Schweitzer Award from the Animal Welfare Institute

primary caregiver and companion through the crisis, every day administering patient care and monitoring their progress. The doctor becomes emotionally involved with the sick animal and experiences mood changes with the ups and downs of their recovery. There is a celebration when the animal survives the ordeal and leaves the hospital. There is profound grief when the animal succumbs to its illness and dies. With either outcome, the experience is mentally exhausting. Full recovery creates joy, satisfaction, and, yes, relief that the pet lived. Death creates feelings of sadness and frustration, second-guessing, and loss of confidence. In this book, we bring those feelings to the surface as I describe my emotional responses to the ups and downs of each animal's medical journey. We hope that veterinarians and their staff find a sense of commonality in these stories and the effect the animals had on my staff and me. Sharing clinical experiences, whether good or bad, brings us together as a profession and helps ease the stress and strain of being a vet.

To give readers a realistic idea of how sick the animals in this book were, I have described the nature of their illness or injury in some detail. The descriptions are graphic and could be disturbing to some. But to be true to the animal's story, the details are necessary and serve to make their medical recovery even more remarkable. To be respectful of owners' privacy, in a few of the stories I have changed the names of either the pets or their owners. In all other respects, the stories are authentic and based on a combination of the pets' medical record, interviews with owners after discharge from the hospital, and my own documentation of events from my case files.

I feel privileged to have been a part of the transformative experience that these animals provided, and I feel compelled to tell their stories so that they may inspire others. Even when close to death, their tails still wagged, sending a clear signal that they had no intention of giving up. I hope that readers will appreciate these pets as examples of the power of healing and positive thinking, not only in their animal companions but in their own lives as well.

Chapter 1: Rip

"Dr. Birchard, we have a Labrador retriever coming in as an emergency with a GDV! He's a valuable, pure breed field trial dog from Kentucky, and he's being flown in on his owner's private jet. The owner insists that his surgeon be a board-certified specialist who has experience with this condition. They specifically want Dr. Bill DeHoff to do the surgery. He's a friend of theirs."

The veterinary student on the emergency service waited impatiently to hear my response. Dr. DeHoff, the senior small animal surgeon at Ohio State University, was out of town. Still, I assured her that, although not as experienced as him, I fulfilled the requirements that the owner was demanding. "When the animal arrives, have the emergency doctors and students confirm the diagnosis, stabilize the patient, and keep me updated," I instructed.

On the outside, I tried to appear calm, hiding my rapid heart rate and elevated blood pressure. But my head was spinning, wondering how badly affected the dog was, if the owners realized that transporting him on a plane could make him much worse, and what they would think when they found out a less experienced surgeon than Dr. DeHoff would be doing the surgery.

GDV, or gastric dilatation-volvulus, is a common problem in large dogs. The stomach rapidly fills with gas and then flips over in the dog's belly, causing severe pain, difficulty breathing, and shock. The initial emergency treatment is to remove the gas and fluid from the stomach with a stomach tube or a large needle placed into the stomach through the skin. If the referring veterinarian had not done this, and if the plane didn't have a pressurized cabin, the stomach would become even more distended and increase the dog's chances of dying.

I was in the middle of treating other patients when this news arrived. I had just finished operating on a dog with a congenital disability of the heart, and my next surgery was to remove a large tumor from a dog's jawbone. I had to focus my thinking and put the bloated airborne Labrador in the back of my mind for the time being. I needed to concentrate on my other duties like checking other patients' blood work and reviewing radiographs. Even though the dog had not yet landed at the airport, students and technicians peppered me with questions: When will the Labrador arrive? How sick was he? What would I need for the surgery? When would we do the operation? I told the students and technicians: "Until we know more, just prepare for a standard GDV surgery, and we'll make adjustments as needed when the time comes."

He arrived a short time later, under heavy sedation and with a stomach tube in place. The referring veterinarian had placed a pharyngostomy tube from his throat into his stomach so that the owner could remove the gas during the flight. When he arrived, he was not stable; his vital signs were not normal, and he needed shock treatment. Radiographs of his abdomen confirmed the diagnosis of gastric dilatation-volvulus. Treatment measures were administered to stabilize him and get him ready for surgery.

His name was Rip. His trainer, who lived in Columbus, Ohio, accompanied him to The Ohio

State Veterinary Teaching Hospital, where I worked as a faculty surgeon. The actual owner resided in Kentucky. Rip was a valuable field trial Labrador— one year old and intact (not castrated). Field trial Labradors are athletic dogs bred and trained to perform in competitive events to demonstrate their retrieving skills. Highly successful dogs achieve "Championship" status, which increases their value like blue ribbon show dogs. Young Rip had not competed in any trials yet, but hopes were very high for his performance career. His owners and trainers wanted the highest level of care possible.

I didn't have much time to get to know Rip and his owner before operating on him. GDV is an emergency, and surgery must be done promptly to put the stomach back where it belongs. I examined Rip, but I didn't get a sense of his personality since he was weak and sedated. I spoke with the trainer briefly. He knew about GDV; he'd been a dog trainer his whole life and knew a lot about dogs and their illnesses. I also spoke with the owner in Kentucky. Although he loved Rip, he was concerned about how all this would affect his career as an athlete.

Both the owner and trainer seemed to resign themselves to the fact that a "junior" surgeon would be caring for their dog. I was one of the younger faculty members of the Veterinary Clinical Sciences Department at Ohio State. I hadn't yet built an impressive reputation and was not well known in the world of veterinary surgery. When an owner demands a specific person operate on their animal and it is not possible, the situation can become awkward. Would they be ready to find fault if something went wrong with the surgery or postoperative care? Operating on a valuable field trial Labrador with GDV was enough of a high-pressure situation without any added reasons for anxiety. There was already tension among the staff surrounding this prized animal.

Rip stabilized quickly after arrival, and we got him anesthetized and into surgery. We prepared him for the abdominal procedure and moved him into the operating room. When I opened his abdomen and examined his stomach, it immediately became clear that this would not be a routine GDV surgery. A large area of his stomach was black, damaged from the severe distension with gas and fluid, which had cut off the blood flow to the stomach. After examining the rest of Rip's abdominal organs and putting his stomach back to its normal location, I proceeded with a partial gastrectomy to remove the dead portion. About 30 percent of his stomach had to be removed. A gastropexy, or tacking procedure, was then done to anchor his stomach in its usual position and prevent further episodes of GDV in the future.

After completing the surgery and getting Rip into the recovery area, I spoke with his trainer and the owner. I told them honestly that the prognosis for survival was not good when the stomach has that kind of damage resulting from the GDV. I promised that we would do everything possible to support Rip, but the truth was he might not make it. I felt bad delivering this news, as they might have been skeptical about hearing it from this "wet behind the ears" surgeon. But they both responded in a concerned but trusting manner, asking me to keep them updated and to do all we could for Rip. We wrote intensive care treatment orders and monitored him closely for complications.

The following day, my students and I did rounds, including examining Rip and assessing his progress. He looked weak and still somewhat sedated but otherwise was stable and comfortable. We updated his treatment orders for the day, finished rounds, and called Rip's trainer with a progress report. "So far so good," I said, "but he's not out of the woods yet."

Over the next couple of days, Rip gained strength and steadily improved. The more I spent time with him, petting and talking to him, I began to appreciate what an affectionate and outgoing dog he was. He loved people and wanted to please them. His slow but persistent tail wag symbolized his general attitude. Beyond his personality, he also had a fantastic physique. He was tall, long-legged, muscular, jet-black in color with a shiny coat and a well-proportioned and handsome head. In a word, he was gorgeous, one of the best-looking dogs I had ever seen. He was obviously physically strong; over the next several weeks I would discover just how strong his spirit was as well.

A Setback

Our plan for Rip was to send him home a few days after his surgery. But when we examined him the morning of postoperative day three, he obviously did not feel well. He suddenly stopped eating, was lethargic, and had a fever. He seemed uncomfortable, especially in his belly. Radiographs of his abdomen showed fluid accumulation. A fluid sample was obtained and analyzed and showed septic peritonitis evidenced by white blood cells and bacteria. Rip was probably leaking from his stomach incision. The highly acidic stomach contents, although fine within the confines of that large saccular portion of the digestive system, if spilled to the outside stomach fluids are incredibly damaging to the tissues in the abdominal cavity. Rip's belly had become an abscess full of pus; we had to reoperate immediately.

I called Rip's trainer and owners and gave them the bad news. I recommended we reoperate on Rip to fix the leaking incision. They, of course, said to do whatever was necessary for him. They were not concerned about the cost, just worried about Rip.

After placing Rip under anesthesia and preparing his abdomen for sterile surgery, we re-opened him using the same incision in his belly. My suspicions were confirmed—his stomach incision was leaking due to more tissue death after his initial surgery, leading to poor healing and rupture of the stomach. I was forced to remove even more of his stomach and re-stitch the healthy tissues back together. We flushed the abdomen with sterile saline solution to remove the pus and stomach contents that had leaked out. Then we placed a drain tube to allow removal of any additional fluid after surgery and closed him up. I called the owners and trainers and told them I was concerned about how Rip would respond to this setback; peritonitis is a severe complication. His chances of making a full recovery were no better than 50/50. I assured them we would do everything we could with supportive care, but sometimes even with attentive support, those patients can still deteriorate. They understood and, of course, were worried, but certainly were not going to give up on Rip.

Again, a concern of the owners was how all this would affect Rip's performance as a field trial dog. Even though he had now lost about half of his stomach, if he survived, I thought he should have been able to function and maintain his weight. To what degree it would affect his stamina and learning abilities were yet to be determined.

I kept worrying about the owner's attitude— would he judge me harshly and begin to lose confidence in me because of the complication that had developed? Outwardly he was polite and supportive, but deep inside, did he regret that Dr. DeHoff had not done the initial surgery? Although these insecurities entered my mind, I had to do everything possible to maintain objectivity and make good decisions for Rip. I focused on the things I could control, his medical care, and the communication with the owner. The rest was up to Rip.

Rip bounced back more slowly from this second surgery, but he did make gradual progress over the next three to five days. Initially, his demeanor was sluggish, but he gained strength and perked up day by day. A saving grace for Rip was that his appetite returned quicker than usual after this kind of surgery. His nutritional intake, a critical factor in recovery from peritonitis, rebounded well, and within a few days, he was eating and seemed to be well on the way to a full recovery. Little did we know Rip's saga was nowhere near over.

As Rip recovered from surgery and grew stronger, so did my relationship with him. I gradually fell in love with this splendid creature. Doctors are instructed to keep a certain distance from their patients to stay objective in their decision-making. My personal history makes that difficult to do. Like many other people, I grew up in a dysfunctional family with an alcoholic father and a mother who, in her confusion, enabled my father's drinking. As a result, I live with a perpetual striving to achieve combined with a deep need for connection and affirmation. Simply put, I'm a sucker for a dog's wagging tail. I find the affection of an animal deeply healing even though I am supposed to maintain emotional boundaries as a doctor.

Maintaining emotional distance was not realistic for Rip and me. We were fighting this battle together. Each day when I did rounds in the ICU, as soon as he saw me, his tail started slowly wagging, a steady thump, thump, thump on the floor. Even when he was too weak to stand and could barely move any part of his body, his tail still wagged. That simple sign of his attitude and friendship was all it took to brighten my outlook make me feel even more bonded to him. I spent a lot of time petting, scratching, and massaging his muscles to help relieve his discomfort from the surgeries.

Like his recovery from the first surgery, Rip made steady progress each day. He had been in the Intensive Care Unit since being admitted to the hospital, but he was not in a cage. The staff made him a large bed on the floor to get to him easier for his frequent medications, intravenous fluids, and monitoring of vital signs. A low, lightweight plastic fence surrounded him. For most dogs, being in an open area like this would not work since as soon as they felt good enough to walk, they would try to leave the designated area and roam around the ICU room. Rip had no interest in doing that and was happy to stay in his place until taken out for walks.

Something Died Inside

Disaster struck again on day three after the second surgery. Once again, Rip stopped eating, developed a fever, and became lethargic and depressed. The fluid coming out of his abdominal drain was discolored, and there was more of it. Abdominal radiographs showed fluid and a large mass filling almost the entire abdominal cavity. Blood tests showed evidence of severe infection and anemia. It wasn't clear what the problem was this time, but we would have to operate yet again.

This news was a blow to everyone's morale— doctors, students, technicians, and of course, the owners and trainers were all distraught about this recent development. After the second surgery, we all thought that with Rip's steady improvement, he was "home free." Why was he developing more problems in his belly? Was the stomach incision leaking again? Had more stomach tissue died? Or was it just worsening of his infection? The owners asked all the same questions again: Would Rip live through this? Would he still be able to train and compete as a field trial dog? What would his quality of life be like? I couldn't give them many answers this time; Rip was taking us into unknown territory. All we could do was operate again, see where the problems were, and do our best to fix them.

Rip was taken back to the surgical area and anesthetized. His abdomen was prepared, and he was moved to the surgical suite. We again went into his belly by simply taking out the previously placed stitches—this was becoming a routine procedure for Rip, now having his third surgery since being admitted. His abdomen was familiar territory for us.

What we found was completely unexpected and something I had never seen before or since. The omentum, the large fatty, vascular, and lymphatic-rich membrane surrounding and protecting the internal organs, had died. It was black like the damaged stomach that we had removed several days ago. The blood vessels had all developed blood clots and ceased to function. It was one of the ugliest things I had ever seen. The usually silky, slippery, yellowish pink sheet covering the organs was a blue-black, cold, cadaveric alien corrupting Rip's body. I couldn't get it out fast enough.

After removing the omentum, we again flushed Rip's abdomen with sterile saline and sutured him up. His abdominal muscles were becoming hard, thick, fibrous, and inflamed from all the opening and closing of his belly and the intermittent infection and the surgical trauma. The abdomen is not supposed to be invaded so many times in so few days. Because we had now operated on Rip three times, the tissues were stuck in the initial phase of wound healing, perpetually inflamed and not permitted to progress to the next stage. Once we could leave his belly alone and the healing got back on track, the tissues could begin to knit together and gain some strength.

Thump, Thump, Thump

Rip did not bounce right back from this episode. He was weak, couldn't stand up, and had no appetite. Life-sustaining tubes and catheters crawled in and out of his body. He was in critical condition. When I entered the ICU and he saw me, not one muscle on his body moved, except, of course, his tail. He still mustered enough strength to give me that slow, deliberate, tail wag . . . thump, thump, thump. Beaten down by disease, trauma, infection, and death of internal organs, he still managed to wag his tail. His spirit had been damaged but was not dead. There was still life in this fantastic, beautiful creature. He was not giving up, and neither were we.

Now at a much slower pace, Rip gradually improved. Day by day, his vital signs improved, his appetite returned, and he got stronger. We made it a whole week without a catastrophe, then another week. He was starting to act like a normal dog, eating well, increasingly active, and playful, and showing us his engaging and affectionate personality. Although we knew we would miss him terribly, we felt that he had finally recuperated enough to send home. I was comfortable with this decision since the Columbus-based trainer would take him to his home for a few weeks where he could continue his rehabilitation. Being close to Ohio State would be ideal to follow his progress.

A Chance to Celebrate, But Too Soon?

Shakespeare wrote, "When sorrows come, they come not as single spies, but in battalion." We were about to experience that truth once again.

After Rip was home for several days, Jack, the trainer, decided he and his wife would host a reception for all the doctors, staff, and students who had cared for him during his hospitalization. It was a wonderful gesture of thanks, and of course, we were eager to see Rip again.

It was a fun get-together; we were able to relax and talk about Rip's ordeal and his incredible recovery from so many major operations and complications. We spent time with Rip in more pleasant surroundings. His trainer gave us a brief education about the world of field trial dogs with many pictures and demonstrations of the training and how the actual trials are done. It is a world unto itself, and I enjoyed learning more about it. Being a veterinarian does not mean you know everything about the world of dogs, such as show dogs and competitive dogs. We're not taught much about that in vet school.

When I initially spent time with Rip that night, I thought he looked pretty good. He had gained weight, his coat was shiny and full, and his activity and attitude were good. But there was a problem. After running around playing with everyone, he laid down to rest. I noticed that his breathing was just a little too rapid and mildly labored. He was over-expanding his chest when he inhaled. His breathing wasn't normal. I didn't want to put a damper on the spirit of the party, but I pulled Jack aside and quietly told him we'd better get Rip back into the clinic for a recheck exam and chest radiographs. I didn't know what the problem was, but I was concerned. Little did I know that yet another chapter in Rip's medical saga was about to be written.

The next day, Jack brought Rip to the OSU hospital, familiar territory for both. Rip didn't seem to mind being back in the place where he had suffered so much. Always playful and happy, he was oblivious to his surroundings. We performed a physical examination which was unremarkable except for his chest. Listening through a stethoscope, the lung and heart sounds were muffled, not the clear, crisp sounds usually heard. Something in the chest cavity was pushing the surface of the lungs away from the interior of the chest wall, making it harder to hear them. We saw fluid in the chest cavity on radiographs, a lot of it. It was surprising that he was breathing so well considering the fluid pushing on his lungs.

We drained some of the fluid from his chest with a syringe and needle. The fluid looked like milk, white and creamy. It looked like someone had poured whole milk into his chest. We drained a quart of it from each side. Analysis of the fluid showed that Rip had chylothorax. In this rare condition, the lymphatics in his chest cavity were leaking a fatty, protein-rich fluid normally transported from the intestine to the heart via a structure called the thoracic duct. Instead of emptying into his bloodstream, the fluid leaked into his chest cavity, and his lungs were being bathed in it. It was a serious setback. Everyone was devastated.

We didn't know why he developed this unusual problem. Coincidentally, chylothorax was an area of research interest for me. For several years before treating Rip, I researched the causes and best treatment for chylothorax. Although I was concerned about Rip and felt terrible that he had to battle yet another problem, I was familiar with the disease and was eager to use the techniques I had developed in my studies to help him.

I explained the situation to Jack and Rip's owner. Like me, they could not believe that Rip had to overcome yet another complication. They had many questions: Why did this happen, is it curable, how will it affect him, and again, what does this mean for his future as a field trial dog? I tried to answer their questions, but there were many uncertainties. It's such a rare disorder. "I don't know" was the best I could offer for many of their queries. Although this was another opportunity for the owner's trust in me to diminish, he remained steadfast in his support. We had come this far, and he wasn't giving up on Rip or me. We discussed the plan of action, which included another major operation. They told me to go ahead.

The surgery for the treatment of chylothorax is delicate and tricky. It involves making separate incisions to open both the abdomen and thorax. It's a big operation for a dog or cat that has never had surgery before, let alone a dog recovering from three major surgeries. There were risks and potential complications: anesthetic problems, infection, healing issues, and accidental trauma to vital nerves and blood vessels. But without the surgery, Rip's chances of recovery were low, so the benefit of the operation outweighed the risks.

The first step was to get Rip safely under anesthesia—not an easy proposition considering the fluid in his chest that compromised his breathing. We drained as much fluid as possible with a syringe and needle. We then placed him under anesthesia with a tube in his trachea to put him on a ventilator to assist his breathing. The entire right side of his body was then clipped and scrubbed for surgery. Every time we had to shave him for surgery, now his fourth procedure, it was sad to remove the beautiful, shiny deep black hair from his body. The scar on his belly from the previous three invasions of his abdomen reminded us of his recent medical saga.

He was moved to the operating room, placed on the table, and covered with sterile drapes. The first step was to make a small incision on the side of his abdomen to view his lymphatic vessels and place a tiny catheter into one of them. Liquid contrast material that can be easily seen on radiographs was then injected through the catheter to illuminate the lymphatic vessels. The procedure is called lymphangiography, and the purpose is to identify where the milky fluid was leaking from and determine how to stop it.

The lymphangiogram showed that Rip had a blockage of the thoracic duct, the main pathway for lymph to drain from the intestines to the large vein that empties into the heart, the vena cava. The obstruction developed due to the intravenous catheters he had in his jugular veins for so many weeks when he was treated for the GDV and subsequent complications. Even though those catheters had been removed many days ago, they caused blood clots to form in the vena cava. The obstruction was causing a backup of fluid in the lymphatics; the increased pressure in the vessels caused fluid to leak out and accumulate in his chest cavity, causing his abnormal breathing.

We had to tie off the thoracic duct upstream from the leaking area to stop fluid accumulation in his chest. From the results of my research, we knew that ligating the duct near the diaphragm would force the lymph fluid to find a new pathway to the bloodstream in the abdomen, bypassing the chest. Thoracic duct ligation requires a surgical incision into the chest cavity. Delicate dissection and placement of a suture to ligate the thoracic duct is performed. It sounds easy, but the thoracic duct lies just above the aorta, the largest artery in the body.

Injury to the aorta during the dissection would cause catastrophic hemorrhage and immediate death. I took deep breaths, slowly isolated the duct, and carefully placed the suture ligation. It went fine. We all had a sigh of relief and continued. We placed a tube in Rip's chest to drain fluid and air, and then closed his incisions. Now we could only wait and see if the surgery was successful.

The next day Rip was pretty "dopey" from his pain medications, but his vital signs were good, and he seemed comfortable. Again, when he saw me he didn't stand up, but his tail made the characteristic slow wag, thump, thump, thump. He was tired, sore, and drugged but not defeated. As the day wore on, he started getting up, walking around, and even began eating a little bit of food—what a remarkable dog. In two months, he had four extensive operations involving both body cavities. The chances of him surviving all these complications had been slim, maybe a 5-10 percent chance of making a full recovery. But he persisted. After a few more days in the hospital, we were able to disconnect Rip from his array of tubes, catheters, and monitors and send him back to Jack and Judy for continued recovery and rehabilitation. We saw him again two weeks after the last surgery. His incisions had healed, and he was getting his strength back, gaining weight, becoming more active, and maintaining his puppy-like behavior. Chest radiographs showed no more fluid in the thoracic cavity. He was shaved and scarred but still beautiful.

Unexpected Gift

Over the next few months, Rip gradually went back into field trial training. He started having some success as an athlete. He returned to Kentucky to live with John and Marie, the breeders who had brought him into the world. Everyone was amazed that this incredible dog, who'd fought through a series of life-threatening issues, was not only alive but competing and doing well. They would periodically call or write me letters to tell me how "Ripper," as they called him, was doing. A couple of years after he was released from the hospital, they called me just before Christmas with the news that Rip had fathered a litter of puppies, and would we like to have one? My family and I were delighted. We named her Daisy. She was gorgeous like her father, had the same loving personality, and was a part of our family for twelve years. She was obsessed with retrieving, not surprising considering her genetic background. Every time I looked at her, I couldn't help but think about her father, the dog with the most incredible will to live that I had ever seen.

Many years later, I received a letter from John and Marie. At ten years of age, Rip died suddenly from unknown causes. The note summarized his life from puppyhood to his medical ordeal, his training, retirement from competition, and the circumstances surrounding his death and burial. They emphasized how special a dog he was, his effect on people, and how there seemed to be a purpose for his life. Although he never excelled in competition, he inspired people with his energy and affection.

He also inspired me. So many times during his illness he could have given up and let the life slowly drain out of him. So many times I considered recommending euthanasia to the owners. But then I would walk back to the ICU, and that tail would do the slow thumping wag. It was his way of telling me that where there's life, there's hope. He never lost the one essential element of life: his spirit. Something more potent than medical care was at work. He was meant to survive; I just needed to support the unfolding of his life's purpose.

Noted physician, surgeon, and author Dr. Richard Selzer said that a person's soul becomes evident during illness; the wound is a window to the spirit.[5] I had many opportunities to see Rip's soul, and what I saw changed me as a surgeon and person. From a medical standpoint, I learned that a dog could survive four surgeries in a matter of a few months and still recover completely. From an emotional perspective, I realized that keeping the spirit alive and deciding to fight rather than submit can sustain me when times are tough. At times I felt so sorry for Rip, and I wondered if only I had done a better job caring for him, maybe he would have recovered quicker or wouldn't have developed so many complications. But instead of looking back and second-guessing my decisions, his positive attitude kept me looking forward, helping him overcome the setbacks and fully recover. Rip did not know or care that I was a "junior" faculty member who was still learning and didn't have all the answers. He just knew that I was his caregiver and companion. Together we completed the journey. Although never a champion field trial dog, Rip had an even more significant impact on the world—by giving me confidence in my abilities, he indirectly affected thousands of animal patients that came after him. For this, he deserved so much more than trophies or blue ribbons. He deserved love, and that he gave and received his entire life.

As I shared earlier in this chapter, it's in my nature to strive, excel, and even compete. This motivation has served me well in many ways and helped me have a very satisfying career as a veterinary surgeon. Rip reminded me that other qualities in my life are of equal importance, things like dedication, compassion, and perseverance in the face of difficulty. It's not about winning and losing— it's about giving and receiving love. I can never thank Rip enough for teaching me these life lessons.

Chapter 2: Hershey

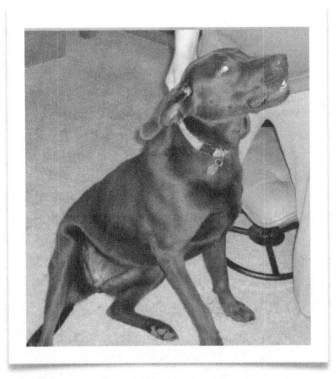

When the weather was good, Hershey's owners let her spend most of the day in the backyard. She loved being outside in the fresh air and sunshine. Every day when they got home from work, she would make a beeline to the back door to welcome them home. There was joyful dancing, tail wagging, and eager anticipation of her evening meal.

But this day was different. When they arrived, she wasn't at the door. They opened the door and called her name. She slowly walked toward them in the yard with her head down and tail tucked. As she came into the house, they noticed some blood on her rear end. They looked out in the backyard near the perimeter fence and were shocked by what they saw.

It looked like a crime scene. There was blood everywhere. Hershey, an eight-month-old female chocolate Labrador, had been viciously attacked by two other large dogs. She had been in her own backyard when the dogs from the neighbor's yard crawled under the fence, came into her property, and attacked her. They grabbed her in the rear and thighs. She was trying to escape their powerful jaws and teeth when they jumped her. When her owners examined her more closely, they discovered several open flesh wounds.

Hershey's owners immediately took her to their veterinarian for treatment. The damage was severe, with many bite wounds in the skin of several areas of her body and damage to the deep layers of tissue, including muscle and tendons. Hershey received supportive care and wound treatment at the vet's clinic. But he immediately knew that she would need a lot of intensive care, more than he could offer at his clinic. The veterinarian personally drove her to the Veterinary Teaching Hospital at The Ohio State University to be admitted for assessment and treatment.

Hershey was seen by the Emergency Service at Ohio State, and she was examined and evaluated with blood tests and other diagnostics. The emergency doctors found her depressed, dehydrated, and in pain. Her wounds were extensive, covering about 30 percent of her body. On the initial assessment, no injury to internal organs was evident. She was admitted to the hospital and given intravenous fluids, antibiotics, and medication for pain. A continuous intravenous infusion of fentanyl was administered for pain. Fentanyl is one of the most potent narcotic analgesics used in veterinary and human medicine. Hershey needed it.

After a few hours, when she was more stable, the emergency team placed Hershey under anesthesia and carefully examined her wounds. The area of trauma on her body and legs was clipped, cleaned, and flushed with sterile saline. Dead tissue was surgically removed (debridement). More than fifty skin punctures were found on her body, and there was a severe injury to the deep muscles and tendons of her left rear leg. Her back, the base of her tail, and the perianal area also suffered deep tissue trauma. Some of the muscle in her legs was torn apart and already turning black, obviously dead due to loss of blood supply. Many areas of the skin were also black, and other significant areas were severely bruised and inflamed. Like most wounds that occur from bites, the skin was pulled up and separated from the underlying layer of tissue. The subcutaneous fat, fascia, and muscle were macerated when the attacking dogs tried to shake Hershey while biting her. This trauma to the deep layers is the most dangerous aspect of this kind of injury. When extensive deep wounds get infected, the bacteria can spread to the bloodstream through the damaged tissues and the entire body. Bacteria in the blood is called sepsis, or blood poisoning. Sepsis usually results in the death of the patient.

Hershey was placed in the intensive care unit to continue her supportive care and monitoring. She had a rough night, but gradually her vital signs stabilized. She became more comfortable when the fentanyl started to take effect. The doctors updated Hershey's owners on her situation and all that they were doing for her. They were beside themselves with a combination of anger and sadness that their beautiful dog had been so viciously attacked.

On the Brink

Hershey was transferred to my surgical service the next day. Still groggy from the previous night's anesthesia, she looked beaten and demoralized. She tried to respond to our coaxing and petting but was too weak and sore to move. Her wounds were already severely infected. Pus, the thick pale-yellow fluid that is a combination of bacteria, dead white blood cells, and tissue debris poured out of many openings in her skin. We feared the worst as sepsis waited in the wings like a demon threatening to show its ugly face and terminate Hershey's life.

All wounds go through a phase of inflammation for the first few days after injury. It's an essential part of the healing process, allowing necessary cells, proteins, and other substances to find their way into the wounded tissues. Wounds become infected when the cell damage and bacteria overwhelm the body's defense mechanisms. The result is the classic signs of severe inflammation as described by the Latin terms: rubor (redness), calor (heat), tumor (swelling), and dolor (pain). These signs were evident on Hershey's back, tail, rear end, and left leg.

We continued treating Hershey with intravenous fluids for hydration, antibiotics to combat infection, and potent pain relievers. Blood tests were repeated, and her serum proteins were low, probably from loss of protein from the wounds. This represented a potentially major problem since Hershey would need a lot of protein to rebuild her tissues. I spoke with Hershey's owners that morning and painted a bleak picture of her prognosis. She was in critical condition, and her chances of survival were no better than 50/50. She would be in the hospital for the foreseeable future. We would have to do daily wound debridement surgery on her, followed by flushing and bandaging. She would also need intravenous antibiotics, intravenous fluids, and analgesic (pain-relieving) drugs. It would be costly.

The owners never wavered—they were committed to doing everything possible for Hershey regardless of cost. Like most Labradors, she was a wonderful, loving sweetheart of a dog, and they were not giving up on her. We vowed our commitment to her as well. If we could keep the infection from spreading throughout her body, she would have a chance.

Managing Hershey's pain was a critical part of her treatment. Animals in pain are reluctant to move, which increases the likelihood of pneumonia and bedsores. If uncomfortable, an animal will not eat, delaying their recovery. Pain also interferes with wound healing due to its stress on the body.[6] Hershey received intravenous fentanyl and oral analgesics like non-steroidal anti-inflammatory drugs to help her with the severe pain.

We placed Hershey under general anesthesia and managed her wounds beginning that first day and for many consecutive days after that. The repetitive process was to clean, scrub, surgically remove dead tissue, flush, and bandage. We used a bandaging technique called tie-over bandages. Bandages were placed directly over each wound and secured to the skin with suture loops and laces, like lacing up a shoe. The bandages looked like patches individually covering each wound. It's a much more effective technique for covering the injuries, as less bandage material is used than conventional bandages, and patients are more mobile.

With each episode of debridement, Hershey lost more skin. Daily debridement is a standard procedure in wound management. Some areas of skin take time to "declare" that they are dead or infected. With no chance for survival, the damaged skin needs to be surgically removed. We cut away the black and gray leathery tissues with thumb forceps, scissors, and scalpels each day. The rule of thumb is to cut back to bleeding edges to remove all the dead and necrotic areas, leaving only healthy tissue behind. Without debridement, the dead skin would eventually peel off. But it would take much longer, and the chances of infection would be greater. With the daily surgeries to remove dead and dying tissues, it became clear that Hershey would wind up with two vast areas of open skin wounds. One was the size of a dinner plate on her back near the tail. The other was the size of a saucer on her left thigh over the hamstring muscles.

You Are What You Eat

Even with anesthesia and surgery for the previous seven days, Hershey quickly recovered from each procedure and became more active and even a little playful. She didn't develop a fever, and tests did not show evidence of sepsis. Her attitude never deteriorated. She was happy and wanted attention. She got lots of it from the students and technicians taking care of her and her owners, who visited her often.

A significant factor in Hershey's recovery was that she started eating after a couple of days, and her appetite improved every day. Nutrition plays a vital role in wound healing.[7] The body makes the wounds its top priority—if no nutrients are being consumed, protein will be mobilized wherever available, even robbing it from the blood and organs. In this way, the wound can be like a parasite, draining the body's resources for its own purposes. Hershey's blood protein levels steadily dropped over the first few days of her treatment. Also, when large areas of skin are absent, the exposed flesh loses water, electrolytes, and proteins. Loss of these essential physiologic elements can debilitate patients and make them more susceptible to infection and further injury. By maintaining her appetite, Hershey was sparing her body of this depletion and making a considerable contribution to her recovery. Her serum proteins gradually climbed back to normal after a few days of eating high protein foods.

After several more days, the wounds were progressing enough to discontinue debridement. Hershey no longer needed anesthesia during her wound cleaning and bandage changes. This was a big step forward. Little by little, she was getting "out of the woods." We decided to start changing bandages every other day instead of every day.

But changing the bandages less frequently turned out to be a bad decision. The wounds started to smell bad and began oozing a thick viscous fluid.

The exposed tissues looked pale and yellowish, not the usual bright orange-red color of healthy granulation tissue that fills open skin wounds. Hershey became more lethargic and started losing her appetite. We had taken a step backward.

Prescription for an Infected Wound: Sugar

We went back to daily dressing changes and changed our wound therapy strategy. We started packing granulated sugar in the wounds. Sugar and honey are old-fashioned wound dressing materials that have been used for thousands of years and have regained popularity in both human and veterinary medicine.[8] Sugar draws the infected fluid from the wounds, absorbs it into the bandage, and leaves the wound clean and healthy. Over several hours, the sugar in contact with the tissues becomes liquid. When the dressing is removed, the thick, syrupy fluid gets flushed out with the sterile saline lavage. Fresh sugar is then put on the wound, and the bandage is applied. The hyperosmotic nature of the sugar combats infection, first by drawing pus and bacteria out of a wound and then dehydrating the bacteria and killing them. After a few days of sugar bandages, the wounds looked much better, and Hershey was back to her old self.

Hershey looked good enough now that she could be treated as an outpatient. After 13 days in the hospital, she was released, and the owners brought her in every day for her bandage changes. After several days of sugar treatments, we transitioned to gauze pads impregnated with petroleum jelly. These pads are absorbent but do not have to be changed every day and are not painful to remove. The wounds looked very good in a few more days, and we began to consider closing them surgically.

The first of the open wounds we closed was on the back of her left thigh. Even with the severe damage to the hamstring muscles, Hershey was using the leg with a pronounced limp. She seemed uncomfortable around the open wound on the leg. We were having trouble keeping the bandage on since Hershey was getting more active. I felt that finally getting it closed would be the best decision. The larger wound on her back was still not ready, with gaps in the granulation tissue needing to fill in. We planned to continue bandaging for a few more days.

We anesthetized Hershey and clipped and prepared the leg wound for surgery. After a light debridement of the skin and the deeper layers, we loosened the skin edges by separating them from the underlying scar tissue. We closed the wound in several layers: the deep fascial layer, the middle subcutaneous layer, and then the outer layer of skin. It came together nicely and looked good. Finally, at least one of Hershey's massive wounds was now closed. Hershey was sent home the day after but returned every couple of days for ongoing bandage changes of the other wound.

Slip Me Some Skin

After a week of bandaging, the larger wound on Hershey's back looked good enough to close, but it would be challenging. It was much too big to simply free up the skin edges on each side and bring it together as we had done on her thigh. There wasn't enough skin to do that. If we tried to close it just using the available skin around the wound, it would be so tight it would surely break down (dehiscence), and then we would be right back where we started. Something more complicated would be necessary. We needed to bring healthy skin to the wound by making a flap or a skin graft. We decided on a flap since there was a better chance of success, and the full-thickness skin in a flap would grow much more hair after it healed. The skin flap would look better and protect Hershey from the sun and superficial trauma.

The skin flap we used on Hershey is called a local advancement flap. We free up skin from near the wound and move it to fill in the defect. After inducing general anesthesia, we made two long parallel incisions that extended from the lateral margins of her wound and went up to her back toward her head. Each incision was about eight to ten inches long, and the flap was about twelve inches wide, making it somewhat rectangular. We undermined (separated) the skin and subcutaneous tissues from their deep attachments but left one end of the rectangle attached to Hershey. The undermining is tricky because the blood vessels that nourish the skin must not be injured or else the skin would die. Once freed from the deep fascia, the skin was pulled back toward her tail to cover the wound. Sutures were used to anchor the skin in its new location. Hershey recovered well from anesthesia and was sent home the following day.

Hershey came back in for skin staple removal ten days later. She looked great—the incisions were all healed, she was active and playful, eating well and gaining weight. We removed the staples and sent her on her way. Her owners were overjoyed by her progress. Several months later, I called the owners to check in on Hershey. She was fully recovered and doing very well. I asked the owners to send me some pictures of her to see the result of her skin reconstruction. The photos arrived by email; she looked fantastic. All her hair had grown back in, and you could not even tell where the injury had occurred. She had indeed made a complete recovery.

Three years after her bite wound injuries, Hershey returned to the veterinary hospital at Ohio State. She was lame in her right rear leg (not the one that had been injured with the wounds). The problem was a ligament injury in that leg. She was doing very well in all other respects—happy, in good condition, and still affectionate.

I spoke with the owners at the time of this writing, some twelve years after the attack. They said that Hershey is still doing well and suffered no permanent after-effects other than being slightly sensitive around her tail's base. We spoke at length about the entire experience of her trauma, and they said it was the most emotionally traumatic event they had ever experienced. The owner got choked up as he described the graphic scene of her leaving a trail of blood in the yard. As I mentioned in the Preface, a medical crisis like Hershey's significantly strengthens the bond between owner and animal. Hearing her owner talk about her twelve years later made it clear that she continues to be a vital member of their family and a valued friend.

Hershey was a fantastic patient with a spirit all her own. She survived massive trauma from two large, aggressive dogs that mangled her body. Bite wounds usually become infected since dogs' mouths are teeming with bacteria (don't believe the mythology that their mouths are cleaner than humans'). These bacteria are injected deep into tissues during the fighting. The traumatized tissues are a perfect environment for bacteria to multiply and cause infection. Hershey walked a dangerous tightrope for several days after being attacked and spreading of infection into her bloodstream seemed imminent. Her immune system functioned well, and with the help of supportive care and aggressive wound management, she fought it off.

Hershey is a loving, happy, affectionate dog who invited everyone to be her companion. Her will to live coupled with owners dedicated to her survival combined to allow her medical saga to end well. She taught me that a dog could sustain a hideous injury and emerge unscathed. I learned a lot from Hershey, both medically and spiritually, and I've used that knowledge to benefit many other patients that came after her. When I give continuing education lectures to veterinarians, I frequently use Hershey as a case study to share all that we learned from her. I also wrote an article about her on my educational blog: https://drstephenbirchard.blogspot.com/2014/02/this-is-what-happens-when-labrador.html. (Warning: the images of Hershey's wounds and surgical procedures are graphic and could be disturbing; viewer discretion is advised.)

Hershey was one of the first patients I used sugar on as a wound treatment. Although there was ample evidence supporting its use in the clinical literature, I was still a little anxious about using it since it was new to me. We needed to reverse her tissue infection before she became septic. The sugar bandages worked beautifully, and my concerns quickly faded. I also felt it was a gamble to close her leg wound. The tissues were not ready to be closed, but she seemed so painful in the leg that I thought it was worth the chance. So many times, I've seen animals with infected wounds that were sutured too soon, resulting in worsening of the infection and lack of healing of the unhealthy tissues. I have always taught students that "patience is a virtue" when treating wounds. Don't expect immediate treatment results. Don't hurry to close them; leave them open for debridement and bandaging until the tissues are ready for closure. With Hershey's leg wound, I was not heeding my own advice. Luckily, it healed fine, and she was more comfortable walking on that leg.

Veterinary and medical students know when their faculty bend the rules and refuse to "practice what we preach." In the classroom, we teach basic principles of medical care. Not adhering to your teachings in treating patients can result in a loss of respect from your pupils and colleagues. I explained my reasoning for closing Hershey's leg prematurely to my students and shared my concerns. I think they understood that sometimes we modify the rules to achieve specific goals for our patients. It may be confusing, but medicine is not an exact science. At times, we must exercise some flexibility in our decision-making.

A seemingly unprovoked attack on a gentle, loving Labrador retriever begs the question, why would something like this happen? We know that dogs can be territorial, but that oversimplifies this situation since the attackers came into Hershey's territory to go after her. Something triggered the aggressive response from one or both dogs. Their pack mentality, typical in hunting wolves, may have played a role in their simultaneous attack. Regardless, Hershey suffered a brutal and painful injury that almost took her life. The trauma was physical and emotional. She and her owners suffered emotionally from the horrible experience. It would have been easy to get lost in the unfairness of an episode like this. But rather than obsess over what caused the fight, we all needed to focus on whatever was necessary to save her life. Hershey and her owners quickly realized that emotional healing would be an essential element of her complete recovery.

Hershey was frequently petted, massaged, played with, and talked to during her prolonged stay in the hospital, and her owners visited her often. I believe she felt loved and supported which were as crucial to saving her life as the fluids, antibiotics, surgeries, bandages, and stitches. Multiple studies have found that gentle touching has medical benefits for animals.[9] Regular petting of sick animals helps their recovery by lowering stress and improving their immune system. The people doing the petting benefit by reducing their own heart rate, blood pressure, and stress. Doctors must never forget that our goal is not just to cure our patients, but also to care for them. The two go hand in hand. If you're a vet, take the time to pet your patients, talk to them, and give them a treat. It will make you both feel better.

Chapter 3: Charlie

We Hurt the One We Love

Things were a bit chaotic at Charlie's home, as the family was in the middle of moving to a new house, and there was much packing and truck loading to be done. Their dog Charlie, a handsome and lovable eight-year-old golden retriever, wasn't sure exactly what was going on but was excited and nervous about all the activity. To keep him from running away during the constant opening and closing of doors, one of the family members hooked him to his leash and looked for a place to tie him up. Not finding a better option, they tied him by his leash to the back bumper of their U-Haul trailer parked in the driveway.

When the packing was done, the family loaded boxes into the trailer. Everyone got in the car and headed down the road. They had traveled about a mile when they stopped at a traffic light. The driver behind them rushed out of his car, ran up to their car and banged on the window. "Your dog's tied to the back of your trailer, and he's seriously hurt!"

The owners were horrified and in shock. They couldn't believe they had made such a terrible mistake. They had completely forgotten that Charlie was tied to the trailer bumper. The car had dragged him on the road for one mile. They jumped out of the car and ran to the back of the trailer. Charlie lay on the road battered and bloody, but still alive. A passer-by had called the police, who quickly arrived on the scene. The police officer was so overwhelmed by Charlie's condition that he offered to put him out of his misery right there by shooting him. The owners declined the offer and gently put him in the car to take him to their veterinarian for emergency treatment.

Charlie was treated for shock at the veterinarian's office with intravenous fluids, corticosteroids, and antibiotics. He was obviously in severe pain and was given potent analgesic medication. He had severe wounds all over his body: all four legs, his head, his chest, and even his lips. The skin was missing from some underlying muscles and bones (known as de-gloving injuries). He didn't appear to have any fractures, but the vet was concerned about nerve damage to his legs. An EKG was performed and showed premature ventricular contractions, a form of abnormal heart rhythm. The veterinarian gave him intravenous lidocaine; a local anesthetic also used to treat problems with heart rhythm. Charlie was fighting for his life; supportive care over the next twenty-four hours would be critical to his survival. The emergency vet also offered euthanasia of Charlie, but the owners again declined. They were going to do everything possible for him, even if his chances of survival were poor. They hoped and prayed that by some miracle, Charlie would not die because of their terrible mistake.

Charlie spent the night at the vet's office, and, amazingly, he made it through the night. The emergency veterinarians had done well keeping him alive, but they also knew he would need advanced surgical care over the next several weeks, so they referred him to the Veterinary Teaching Hospital at The Ohio State University. The veterinarian personally drove him to the university clinic. At Ohio State, Charlie was admitted by the chief surgical resident, Dr. Barb Lightner. Because he couldn't walk, he was wheeled into the hospital on a gurney.

One Bloody Traumatic Wound

Charlie was hospitalized at the OSU clinic on April 1, 1996, over twenty-three years ago at this writing. But even so long ago, I still remember when I first saw him lying there on the gurney in the hallway outside of the examination rooms. I had never seen a dog so horribly injured from head to toe. Virtually his entire body was one terrible, bloody, traumatic wound. As he failed to keep his feet behind the trailer, there were areas where the road had scraped away large chunks of flesh, leaving exposed bone and muscle behind. I went over to him, wanting to console him by petting him somewhere, but it was difficult to find a place to touch him that was not injured. He looked at me with a sad face—he was beaten not only physically but emotionally. Still, he seemed to like being gently touched in a part of his body that wasn't broken. As with Rip, maintaining a certain emotional distance from Charlie was impossible. Even the most cold-hearted person would have been moved by what they saw.

Like everyone else, Dr. Lightner was shocked by his condition. She shook off her emotions, flipped her internal switch to doctor mode, and began to assess Charlie's medical needs and make plans for his treatment. It was not advisable to immediately do a complete physical examination on him; it would have been intensely painful and may have induced shock. But on her brief exam, she found that his vital signs were good, and he was alert and responsive. Charlie was obviously in pain and was very lethargic and non-ambulatory. His heart rate was elevated. An EKG was obtained, and he continued to have ventricular premature contractions, a common finding in recently traumatized animals. The team inserted an intravenous catheter and gave Charlie two injectable antibiotics, intravenous fluids for hydration, and medication for the arrhythmia. Charlie's PCV was low (anemia) on his blood evaluation, probably due to blood loss during the accident. Chest radiographs showed no severe abnormalities. Dr. Lightner planned to administer general anesthesia later that day to perform a complete examination and assess and treat his wounds.

Under anesthesia, Dr. Lightner and her team evaluated all of Charlie's injuries, and there were many. He had serious skin wounds on his left shoulder, both lower front legs, left rear leg, left side of his chest, and the top of his head. Even the right side of his lip was ripped apart. Besides losing the skin over his left knee, the kneecap (patella) had been almost completely sheared off by the road, with only a thin sliver of bone remaining. Radiographs of all his legs were taken, and thankfully no fractures were seen.

All the wounds were clipped, thoroughly cleaned, and debrided. Many of the lacerations were sutured closed. However, some of them, including the massive injury on the left leg that extended from Charlie's flank to below the knee, could not be closed because there was insufficient skin left. Those wounds were left open but covered with bandages. Skin reconstruction with rotating flaps or skin grafts would be necessary to close them sometime in the future. When finished, Charlie's appearance was better, but he still looked like he had been on the losing side of an awful battle. Skin staples and bandages were everywhere. We moved him into the Intensive Care Unit, where he received IV fluids, antibiotics, analgesics, and drugs to control his arrhythmias. An indwelling urinary catheter was placed to monitor his urine production to ensure his kidneys were functioning well. Since Charlie could not stand, the catheter would also prevent him from urinating all over himself for the next several days.

We called Charlie's owners to update them on what was being done for him and how he was doing. The owners were apprehensive about him, especially the pain he was experiencing. They continued to feel awful about the nature of the accident and how their mistake might have cost Charlie his life. We were honest with them—he was one of the most severely injured animals we had ever treated, and he would be fighting several battles in the next few days. Cardiac arrhythmias, pain, and wound infection were the primary concerns. We were doing everything we could to prevent and treat those severe issues. If there was ever a dog classified as being in "critical condition," it was Charlie.

On the second day in the hospital, Charlie looked a little better; he could sit up on his sternum but could not stand and preferred to stay still. He still had a very fast heart rate, but no further arrhythmias were seen overnight. Some of the open wounds were draining some fluid and needed re-bandaging. Just like Hershey in Chapter 2, wound infection leading to sepsis was a significant concern. If the infection spread to the bloodstream, Charlie's chance of survival would be very slim.

Signs of Hope

There was some good news, as Charlie began responding to his name and even wagging his tail.

The veterinary students and nurses were very gentle with him. They gave him lots of tender loving care, which he seemed to appreciate. He had lived another day and was doing slightly better. But when the medication for the cardiac arrhythmias was decreased, the ventricular premature contractions came back with a vengeance. The medication dosage was increased to control the arrhythmias. Charlie had a long way to go and was still in critical condition.

On the third day in the hospital, Charlie's owners came to visit him for a short time. They appreciated the chance to be with him, but seeing his wounds, the staples, bandages, bruising, and swelling reminded them of what a horrible trauma he had suffered. He looked pathetic. Euthanasia had gone through their minds, but they wanted to save him if possible. The expense of treatment was not a concern—they wanted Charlie to receive the highest level of care that we could offer. Overwhelmed with guilt, the tears flowed freely while they gently caressed him and softly said his name. I could not even imagine what they were going through.

Over the next few days, Charlie took some baby steps forward. He was more alert, his heart rate and rhythm were stabilizing, and he even ate a little bit and drank some water. He still could not stand and required intensive nursing care to keep him clean and dry. Overall, his wounds were beginning to heal, but some of the open areas looked infected, just what we did not want to see. Also, additional radiographs obtained of Charlie's abdomen revealed something abnormal in his stomach. We planned a second anesthetic event to do multiple procedures. We did more debridement of his wounds and reconstructed the patellar tendon on his knee. We also did endoscopy of his stomach using a flexible tube with a camera lens at the end. The scope is passed through the mouth to allow doctors to see inside the stomach.

All the procedures went well. Some additional wounds were closed. The open ones were cleaned and debrided to trim away infected tissues. Dr. Lightner re-attached the patellar tendon to the underlying bone to allow the knee to function. We removed a sock from Charlie's stomach with the endoscope. It probably had been there for several days without anyone knowing it. Although the trauma could easily explain his lack of appetite, the sock had not helped matters. He recovered from the procedures well and was ushered back to ICU for continued intensive care.

One Step Forward, Two Steps Back, and a Limp

The second debridement surgery seemed to drain Charlie of his energy. For the next two days, he was more depressed, not eating well, and producing less urine, indicating dehydration. His heart rhythm had normalized, so we discontinued the anti-arrhythmia medication. But he seemed to take a step back, and there was even more trouble developing in one of his legs. When we changed his bandages, his left front leg did not look good. The wounds on upper foot and carpus had been left open and bandaged since there was inadequate skin for closure. He also had injuries over his left elbow and left shoulder. The leg was more swollen, and the tissues looked unhealthy. The foot and carpus were becoming cold to the touch, and Charlie was losing sensation on his foot, indicating possible nerve damage. Losing his front leg would be a problem. With all the extensive wounds over the remaining legs and the significant injury to his left knee, he could not afford to lose a leg. He might never walk again.

We began hydrotherapy on the leg. It was soaked in clean, warm water at each bandage change for the next several days. We also started massage therapy to reduce swelling and stimulate better blood flow to the tissues. It seemed to be helping, but the progress was slow, and doctors and owners alike were still concerned that the leg would not survive. We continued other supportive care measures, such as intravenous fluids, antibiotics, and analgesics. We offered Charlie a variety of foods, but he didn't feel good enough to eat. His lack of appetite was becoming a significant concern. A broken, severely traumatized body needs nutrition to heal.[10, 11] Like Hershey, Charlie needed proteins, vitamins, minerals, and calories to rebuild the injured muscle, tendons, bones, nerves, and skin. If Charlie didn't start eating soon, it could be a life-threatening situation. Charlie's owners were concerned about him. They were beginning to seriously consider euthanasia.

Going Bananas

Three days after the second debridement, we finally saw a glimmer of hope. The owners told Dr. Lightner that Charlie had always liked eating bananas. It seemed odd for a dog to prefer that particular food, but it was worth trying to jump-start his appetite. When offered a nice ripe banana, he eagerly ate the whole thing! A little bit later, he ate six ounces of a prescription canned dog food called A/D. This food is highly concentrated and nutritious, and we frequently give it to convalescing patients. Eating for the first time in five days was a huge step forward for Charlie. His body was finally getting the building blocks needed to heal the wounds. But he would require much more.

The next day, he seemed a little stronger. We changed all his bandages and performed more hydrotherapy and massage therapy on the left front leg, which was no worse than the day before but still very swollen. In the early afternoon, he did it again, ate an entire banana, and then more of the A/D, two whole cans this time. He ate four more cans, another banana, and a cooked chicken breast during the night. Charlie showed us that he wasn't giving up; he was starting to do his part in the recovery process. His appetite improved over the next two to three days, and the questionable leg improved. The swelling was going down, and the color of the tissues looked better. It might not have to be amputated after all.

Although Charlie's appetite had improved, he still was far from eating enough to satisfy the needs of all his traumatized body parts. Therefore, we placed a PEG tube (percutaneous endoscopic gastrostomy), a feeding tube placed directly into the stomach that exits out of the side of the belly. With Charlie under anesthesia, the feeding tube was put in using an endoscope (just like the one used to remove the sock) passed into the stomach through the mouth. The doctor carefully follows a series of steps, putting one end of the feeding tube into the stomach and securing the other end of it to the skin on the abdomen. Canned dog food is mixed with water to make gruel, a thin smoothie consistency, and that gets injected into the tube and travels to the stomach. Dogs and cats tolerate these tubes very well, although they must be covered with a light bandage to prevent them from chewing it out. With PEG tube feedings, we could supplement what he was eating with more food to avoid losing weight and becoming malnourished.

While Charlie was under anesthesia for the PEG tube, we performed more debridement on the open wounds of the left front leg that was still very swollen. While trimming away dead and infected tissues in the foot, we opened an enlarged lymphatic vessel, and a gush of clear fluid came out of the wound. Massage of the paw and lower leg allowed more of this same fluid to pour out and immediately reduced the swelling. The scar tissue forming in the lower leg had obstructed the lymphatics leading to severe swelling of the paw and carpus (lymphedema). The extreme pressure cut off the circulation, making the paw cold to the touch and discolored. Now that we had relieved this pressure, the outlook for survival of the leg seemed to be better. Time would tell.

The next day, Charlie was feeling much better. He was more alert, interactive, and less painful. The front leg was significantly less swollen and had a much better color. He ate well, and the students taking care of him took him outside several times to get some fresh air and sunshine. He still could not stand or walk, but he was finally making some real progress. His owners came to visit, and he ate even more for them. They continued to be concerned but were pleased with his progress.

Charlie had now been in the Ohio State Veterinary Hospital for fourteen days. In that time, he had three wound operations, a sock removed from his stomach, and a feeding tube placed. We had changed his bandages fifteen times. Hydrotherapy and massage therapy had been performed on him every day for the past week. His owners visited him almost every day, sitting with him as he lay on a makeshift bed and spending the time talking to him, petting him, feeding him, and trying to assure him that he would be all right. He had made significant progress. Most of the wounds that were stapled closed at his initial surgery were now healed, so we removed them. None of the injuries appeared to be infected. But he still had sizeable open skin wounds on his left front and left rear legs, and he could not stand up. He still had a long way to go. Charlie would need more surgery and a lot of orthopedic rehabilitation.

Another Piece of the Puzzle

Charlie's next surgery would address the wound on his left knee. It could not be left to heal on its own since it was too large—the resultant scar tissue would make it impossible for him to flex and extend the knee joint (wound contracture). Skin replacement surgery would be necessary, either a large skin flap or skin grafting performed. Dr. Lightner and I put our heads together and decided to perform a skin flap.[12] We would take a long tongue-shaped flap of skin from Charlie's belly and transpose it to the knee. It would remain attached in the groin area, where the blood vessels that supply the flap are located, then rotated to cover the knee and stitched in place on the wound edges. Closing the resulting skin defect on the belly should not be a problem since dogs have plenty of extra skin in this area. But the procedure needed to be done correctly so the skin flap would survive and heal.

We performed the surgery, now Charlie's fourth. We found that the kneecap was loose and unattached to the patellar tendon. Since it appeared permanently damaged, we removed it. The kneecap, or patella, is an integral part of the knee joint that allows the patellar tendon to slide up and down on the femur (thigh bone). We were concerned about the long-term function of the knee without the patella. At least the patellar tendon looked good and was still attached to the tibia.

The day after the skin flap surgery, Charlie seemed lethargic but otherwise was doing well. After four episodes of general anesthesia, it was not surprising that he needed some time to recover fully from this one. His skin flap was predictably swollen and bruised but not more than expected. Charlie took another baby step forward and urinated outside from a standing position. Of course, he didn't hike his rear leg up when he did it, but he was able to squat slightly and urinate on his own. Although a minor step in his progress, it was cause for celebration. Hope springs eternal—watching a canine patient urinate for the first time from a standing position is oddly gratifying for a veterinarian.

Two days after the skin flap surgery, more progress. The flap looked good, and it appeared that we would achieve a complete "take" of the transferred skin to the knee. Charlie's attitude was better; he was much brighter and more active. He also ate enough that he didn't need any supplemental food given through his PEG tube. But most importantly, he started walking. He took several steps outside with some assistance and was visibly quite proud of himself. Not only was Charlie not giving up, but he was taking steps forward in his recovery.

Over the next several days, Charlie's improvement became more rapid and substantial. He was getting stronger, could stand for long periods and take more steps with less assistance. His appetite was excellent, his skin flap was slowly becoming less swollen and bruised, the left front leg was much less swollen, and the paw and carpal wounds were healing well. About a week after the skin flap surgery, he looked so good that Dr. Lightner considered sending him home to his owners within a few days.

Charlie was now making visible progress daily. His open wounds had healed enough to do bandage changes every other day. His appetite continued to be very good, and each day, he walked a little more on his own. All aspects of his condition were improving except for a new problem—he developed a pressure sore, or decubital ulcer, on his right elbow. He had been lying down in his cage for over three weeks, and with the problems with the other front leg, he was putting all his weight on the right elbow. The compression of the skin caused the tissue over the elbow to become damaged, leaving an open wound with the bone of his elbow exposed. In people, these wounds are called bed sores, caused by prolonged convalescence in bed due to severe injury or illness. The elbow ulcer would require bandaging and possibly surgery. Charlie didn't need this added

75

problem, but he kept up his positive attitude—he wasn't going to let this new problem get him down.

Before going home, Charlie needed one more anesthesia and minor surgery. We removed his PEG tube and intravenous catheter, debrided the elbow ulcer, and sutured it closed. Decubital ulcers over the elbow in dogs are notorious for poor healing, and a simple closure without a skin flap or graft may not work. But it was worth a chance to try a simple, less prolonged surgery considering all that Charlie had been through thus far.

Love, Forgiveness, Healing

Twenty-seven days after being admitted to the Ohio State Teaching Hospital, we discharged Charlie to his owners. They were thrilled to get him home. He would still need a lot of outpatient care that included frequent bandage changes on the wounds that were not yet completely healed. But he could be in his surroundings with his family, who would provide him with love and care. He was still receiving medication for pain, but all other drugs had been discontinued since they were no longer necessary. Sending Charlie home was quite an event at the hospital. Many hospital employees, doctors, technicians, students, and even office workers knew Charlie and had followed his progress while in the hospital. Many of them gathered to watch him walk out the door, something that had seemed impossible just a few weeks earlier. He still had a long way to go before being completely healed, but he had made fantastic progress.

Over the next several weeks, Charlie was treated as an outpatient, coming into OSU about twice a week for bandage changes and wound treatments. Although doing well overall, he would still have many "bumps in the road" to contend with in the months ahead. There were still open wounds on all his legs, although they continued to get smaller by wound contraction. This healing mechanism occurs when granulation tissue acts like smooth muscle and pulls the skin edges together to make the wound smaller. In some cases, wound contraction allows for complete wound closure, precluding additional surgery.

The wound that continued to be a concern was on his left front leg, the leg that for a time had appeared as though it might have had to be amputated. Intermittent swelling still occurred but was not as bad as it had been while Charlie was hospitalized. His carpus (wrist) not only suffered skin loss, but the tendons and ligaments in the joint were damaged by the trauma, making the joint unstable. When he put his foot down, he could not bear total weight on that leg because of the instability and pain in the joint. We were considering further surgery to fix the issue, but for the time being, we were supporting the carpus with a splint and having his owners give him pain medication as needed.

The decubital ulcer on his right elbow became a problem. Because he had less pain in his right front leg, he rested on it more, putting more stress on the elbow. Although we debrided and sutured the elbow wound, it became infected and started to dehisce (break open due to poor healing). We continued a bandaging regimen on the leg, but it looked like another major surgery would be necessary for the ulcer to heal.

There was good news and bad news on Charlie's hospital visit two weeks after he was sent home. His left carpus was becoming more stable, and he was bearing more weight on that leg. Surgery to stabilize the joint might not be necessary after all. But the skin on the elbow ulcer had now opened, was not healing, and would need to have surgery. His elbow was painful, and he was becoming lame in the leg. Charlie was re-admitted to the Ohio State hospital, and Dr. Lightner performed a skin flap procedure like the one we had done on his left knee, an axial pattern skin flap.[12] She made a rectangular section of skin from his shoulder region and rotated it to cover the elbow. It was sutured in place, and a well-padded bandage was applied to protect the flap. Also, during that anesthesia, she amputated one of his toes on his left rear leg because a small area of bone was exposed, preventing that wound from healing.

Charlie recovered nicely from his fifth surgery in as many weeks. He went home the day after and continued the twice-a-week outpatient visits for several more weeks.

Charlie continued to improve. His strength was returning, and this, combined with more stability in his joints and less pain in his legs, made him want to be more active. But it was still too soon to allow unrestricted activity, so he just had to be patient. Too much exercise too soon could jeopardize his long-term recovery or at least delay his return to normal function. Considering how he had looked right after the horrific injury, it was amazing that we could even use the phrase "return to normal function."

Free at Last

About two weeks after repairing his elbow wound and amputating his toe, Charlie hit another milestone—all bandages could be removed and did not have to be replaced. Imagine how he felt entirely unencumbered by wraps of cotton, gauze, and tape around his legs. All wounds had progressed enough that the dressings were unnecessary for the first time in two months. In addition, Charlie's care was transferred to his regular veterinarian, who would continue to monitor his progress and oversee his rehabilitation. It was now time for Charlie to increase his exercise and endurance. His owners couldn't have been more pleased.

But Charlie's healing still had one more bump in the road. One month after all bandages were removed, he began licking some of the scars on his left front leg, the one that had almost been amputated because it looked so bad after the injury. A bandage had been misapplied to the leg, with nearly catastrophic consequences. The dressing was placed only on the elbow, not covering the entire leg, and it was too tight. The area below the bandage, including the carpus, became very swollen and oozed fluid through the skin. Charlie's owner brought him back to Ohio State, where Dr. Lightner immediately removed the constricting bandage, performed hydrotherapy on the leg, and placed a proper dressing.

Leg bandages on dogs and cats must always cover the entire appendage, all the way to the toes, regardless of where the skin wound is located. If not, the bandage will slip, constrict the leg, and act as a tourniquet, causing severe swelling and loss of blood flow. Thankfully, Charlie's leg survived due to the quick action of Dr. Lightner and her team. After several days of hydrotherapy, massage, and proper bandaging, the leg was back to normal. He didn't need this complication after all he had been through, but he came through it okay.

Over the weeks and months that followed, Charlie gradually resumed his life as a happy, loving golden retriever. It took several weeks for his hair to grow back over the scars. Although he used all his legs well, he had a slightly abnormal gait when walking and running. This was probably due to the scar tissue in the left front carpus and left knee. But he could do all the things that dogs want to do—run, jump, play, and beg for affection from everyone.

After treating him for his injuries, we didn't see Charlie at Ohio State again for six years. We occasionally heard some news here and there about him, that he was doing well, and his family was enjoying their life with their companion. But he eventually did come back, this time for a much different illness and one that unfortunately would take his life. Charlie had not been eating for about a month, was weak in his rear legs, and had intermittent diarrhea. He was very tired, pale, and dehydrated when he presented to Ohio State. Radiographs and ultrasound quickly found the problem. Charlie had a combination of severe pneumonia and cancer of the liver and spleen. His prognosis was poor—even with intensive care, he would probably only live a few days. The decision for his owners was clear; they elected to have Charlie humanely euthanized. I can't even imagine how difficult a decision it was for them. They were devastated, but they knew it was the right thing to do for their cherished companion.

Charlie is one of the most remarkable stories of recovery from bodily injury that I have ever experienced. His dedicated owners and Dr. Lightner and her team deserve the credit for his incredible recovery. The Ohio State students and technicians spent untold hours nursing Charlie through his healing, and they were essential in his recovery.

Changing his bandages every day, meticulously cleansing his wounds, coaxing him to eat and drink, bathing him after he urinated on himself because he couldn't move, and spending hours sitting with him outside in the sunshine. These were the patient care elements that are often overlooked but every bit as important as the surgeries, medications, and monitoring of vital signs.[13]

Charlie's story would not be complete without talking about his owners and the horrible emotional ordeal they experienced. One can only imagine their overwhelming feelings of guilt and remorse because of his trauma. I spoke with them a few times during visits; Dr. Lightner spent much more time with them and came to know them well. More than a good vet and surgeon, she is a very warm, compassionate person, and she repeatedly tried to console them. It was even more difficult for them when Charlie's clinical situation was critical, and his survival was uncertain. All owners have extreme concern and stress when their beloved pet has a severe illness or is a victim of trauma. But if they feel personally responsible for the pet's suffering, the emotional turmoil can be overwhelming.

Guilt, a familiar feeling for all of us, can be crippling. It can be distracting, make it difficult to think straight, and take the joy out of life. Guilty people tend to self-punish and avoid the person they've wronged.[14] Although challenging, unresolved guilt may be best dealt with by offering an honest apology to the affected person. But in the case of Charlie, how do you apologize to a dog? As painful as it was for them to see Charlie during visits, it was beneficial for him and them to spend time together.[15] Their familiar voices, faces, smell, and touches were immensely helpful to Charlie's healing. They apologized to their companion by surrounding him with their love. Over the years, it has become more evident that this kind of physical contact with loved ones is essential in an animal's recovery from illness or injury.[9] Charlie needed all the love he could get, and so did his owners. They healed each other.

We tried as much as possible to mitigate the family's emotional pain with frequent communication and delivering information as compassionately as possible. The students taking care of Charlie called every day with updates. The owners visited often, almost every day except when he had surgical procedures performed.

Sometimes, the little things can make a big difference in recovery from illness. Early on in Charlie's recovery, he desperately needed to take in nutrients to start the healing process of his broken body. But he was in pain, couldn't move, and in strange surroundings. The stress he was going through robbed him of his appetite, and nothing we offered him seemed to stimulate his interest in food. When his owners were made aware of this, they mentioned that he liked bananas, an odd food item for a dog to crave. They suggested we try feeding him some to see if he would eat something, anything. When the students started feeding him bananas, it seemed to stimulate his appetite and get him eating again. He ate more and more each day, and his body finally received the nutrition it desperately needed. I hope his owners could take some solace in knowing that the information they provided allowed a turning point in Charlie's healing.

Some twenty-two years after we treated Charlie, I spoke with Dr. Lightner about him. We reflected on the miraculous recovery he had made. We both agreed we had learned valuable lessons from him, some of which have helped countless other patients since his ordeal. As Dr. Lightner put it, "Any time I see a badly injured dog, I say to myself, *This looks bad, but it's not as bad as Charlie. Don't give up.*"

Chapter 4: Josie

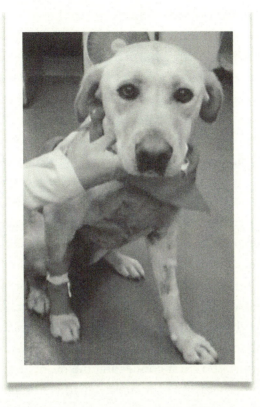

I will never forget October 16, 2007. It was a busy day at the Veterinary Teaching Hospital at The Ohio State University. I had several animals to operate upon that day—a dog with a splenic tumor, a cat with an ear polyp, and a dog with a congenital disability of his liver. I was taking a short break in the hallway between surgeries when Dr. Bob

Sherding called my name from the other end of the hall. Bob was one of the internal medicine faculty members at Ohio State. Usually a very calm person, Bob seemed excited, so his animated behavior was surprising. "Come down here! You've got to look at these radiographs!" I hurried down to where he was. Two radiographs showing two different views of a dog's chest were on the lighted view box. When I looked at the films, my mouth dropped open. "Can you believe it?" Bob asked. No, I couldn't.

My first question to him was: "Is the dog alive?" "Not only alive," he said, "she walked into the clinic with her tail wagging! She's right over there in the triage area." I went over to the exam table she was lying on, where several doctors and students hovered over her. She was a young yellow Labrador, in good condition and fully alert. Her problem was obvious —the shaft of an arrow was protruding from the front of her chest. About eight inches of a black stiff plastic shaft stuck out of the thoracic inlet area, the part of the chest connecting the thorax to the neck. But that wasn't the most remarkable aspect of this dog's injury—the arrow was bouncing up and down at the same rate as her heartbeat.

Seeing the arrow move with every beat of her heart confirmed what we saw on the radiographs. This young retriever had been shot with an arrow that was now entirely through her heart. Miraculously, she was fine otherwise. There was no evidence of bleeding, shock, or other serious problems. I ran back to the view boxes to have another look at her radiographs. They showed no blood or air in the thoracic cavity. It was unreal. How could an arrow have penetrated the heart and not result in catastrophic internal bleeding?

We didn't know anything about her other than the terrible trauma she had suffered. A friend of the shooter had brought her to their local veterinarian right after the incident. The friend claimed it was an accident. The vet quickly assessed her vital signs and then had his technician drive her promptly to Ohio State's emergency clinic for treatment. It was about an hour's drive to Columbus, where the university veterinary hospital was located. The veterinarian wisely did not remove the arrow from her chest by just pulling it out, which would have led to severe bleeding and instant death.

They Called Her Cupid

Until we found her real name, the veterinary students decided to call her Cupid for obvious reasons. After being admitted to the hospital, the emergency doctors and team members evaluated her. They started supportive care: intravenous fluid therapy, antibiotics, and frequent monitoring of vital signs. Results of blood tests performed on Cupid were normal except for an enzyme, creatine kinase, that is elevated when there is an injury to any of the body's muscles. Since the heart is a muscle, this was no surprise.

The veterinary cardiologist at Ohio State, Dr. John Bonagura, carefully performed an echocardiogram on Cupid to assess the damage to the heart. The echo images showed the arrow had entered the right ventricle and exited the left ventricle. In other words, the arrow was entirely through the heart from front to back. The tip of the arrow was sticking out of the left ventricle. Therefore, the arrow had also perforated the inter-ventricular septum, an essential wall of muscle that divides the two ventricles into right and left. An opening between those chambers, called a ventricular septal defect, could cause problems since blood would start flowing, like a short circuit, from one ventricle to the other. Impairment of the pumping function of the heart would result.

There was no bleeding from the heart because the arrow's shaft was sealing the entry and exit holes in the heart. The head of the arrow was a field tip. Bowhunters recognize this as an arrow used for practicing bow and arrow skills by shooting at targets. A broadhead tip is used for hunting. It has razor-sharp triangular blades that slice through whatever it penetrates, causing significant bleeding and damage, killing the hunted animal. The field tip has a sharp point but no cutting blades and is the same diameter as the shaft, thus preventing any bleeding in Cupid.

The emergency doctors immediately sought me out and described the situation with Cupid. I said we needed to take her to surgery immediately. If the arrow somehow became dislodged, there would be life-threatening bleeding and sudden death. It could also cause arrhythmias—abnormal electrical conduction through the heart muscle—which could cause the heart to stop completely. Time was of the essence.

After she was given emergency care, intravenous fluids, antibiotics through an intravenous catheter, and hooked up to an EKG for monitoring, we carefully transferred Cupid to a gurney. We moved her to the pre-surgical room where animals were placed under anesthesia before surgery. She was given a sedative to keep her calm, then an intravenous anesthetic to allow placement of a breathing tube in her windpipe. Anesthesia was then maintained with gas delivered through the breathing tube. The anesthetists worked slowly and carefully to prevent any trauma to the arrow shaft. I was lucky to have an outstanding anesthesiology team working on Cupid. Led by Dr. Rich Bednarski, the highly skilled team did a fantastic job inducing and maintaining anesthesia. Vital signs were monitored closely, including EKG, blood pressure, pulse oximetry, respiratory gases, and others. Having anesthesia personnel you can trust is a tremendous advantage for any surgeon, who can then focus entirely on the surgical procedure.

Conflicting Emotions

After Cupid was anesthetized, the surgical nurses clipped the hair and scrubbed her chest for surgery. While this was happening, I tried to prepare myself for the surgery. I had never done anything like this before. You don't have to be a veterinary surgeon to appreciate the challenge: How do you remove an arrow from a beating heart?

I don't mind admitting that I was a little apprehensive. Questions and uncertainties flew around in my head. What surgical approach should we make to expose the heart? How could we remove the arrow without causing horrible hemorrhage? What if the heart stopped during the surgery? No matter what anyone tells you about the demeanor of surgeons, we are human beings like everyone else, subject to the same feelings, fears, and anxieties that everyone has. But we must keep them under control and prepare ourselves for the job that needs to be done.

I will also admit I was incredibly excited to do the surgery. Surgeons like a challenge, and this one was daunting. A challenging case forces the surgeon to use all their knowledge and skill to complete the necessary task. A heightened sense of engagement with the patient occurs in situations like this. During the surgical procedure, the surgeon has a feeling of being completely immersed in the moment, ignoring all extraneous noise and activity and focusing on the technical details, instructions to the surgical assistants, the instruments, dissection, exposure of the organs, controlling bleeding, and delicately completing each step of the procedure. All these elements and more would be in play during Cupid's operation.

The excitement about the surgery soon spread throughout the hospital like wildfire. Everyone knew about Cupid, and everyone wanted to be involved. Multiple students, interns, and residents begged me to be able to scrub in on the surgery or at least be in the room to watch. I had to deny many of the requests. I'd seen situations like this get out of control—too many people around the operating table and too many people in the surgery room make it impossible for the surgeons and anesthesiologists to hear each other talk. Communication between surgeon and assistants and between surgeon and anesthetist is crucial in a complicated surgery like this one. I selected just the necessary people to assist me with the procedure, promising the rest I would take plenty of pictures for them to see when we were done.

Back to the question: How do you remove an arrow from a beating heart? Here's how we did it.

We carefully moved Cupid into the surgery room, trying hard not to touch the arrow shaft protruding from her body. She was doing very well under anesthesia with good vital signs and parameters. I tried to lighten the mood, saying the arrow would be useful for the anesthesia team—they could monitor her heart rate by counting the arrow's ups and downs per minute!

Cupid was placed on the operating table lying on her back. The surgical approach to the thorax was a median sternotomy. In this approach, after incising the skin, subcutaneous tissues, and the pectoralis muscle, the sternum (breastbone) is cut with an oscillating bone saw. The cut edges are retracted (opened) using a large metal self-retraining retractor. The median sternotomy would give us the best exposure of the entire heart, which we needed to remove the arrow. The same approach is frequently used in people undergoing open-heart surgery.

The Purse String

My team and I scrubbed in, donned our sterile gowns and gloves, and gathered around Cupid on the surgical table. Although everything was happening quickly, we had taken a few minutes as a group before anesthetizing Cupid to discuss our plan for the surgery. I had a few ideas about how I would remove the arrow without causing severe bleeding, but which technique to use would depend on what we found when we exposed her heart. Right now, we just concentrated on safely getting into the chest cavity to assess the damage.

The initial incisions were made, and I began cutting through the sternum with the saw. The anticipation grew as we got closer to being inside the chest cavity. Even though things were going well thus far, I realized there was something different about me. My hands were trembling. I've never had problems with trembling hands during surgery, but I was so excited about doing this operation it was giving me the shakes! My resident must have noticed because she said under her breath, "Everything is going well, and you're doing fine." I needed to calm down, be deliberate and systematic, and let my hands flow through the procedure. After a few deep breaths, my heart rate decreased, and the trembling stopped.

Finally, we had Cupid's chest opened, the retractors in place, and the heart exposed. You could hear a pin drop in the operating room. We saw a perfectly normal beating heart completely skewered by a smooth black rod. As predicted by the echocardiogram, the arrow had entered the chest through the thoracic inlet, penetrated the right ventricle, went all the way through, and exited the left ventricle. We could see the arrow tip sticking out of the left side of the heart. Amazingly, the lungs were untouched, no other blood vessels were injured, and there was not a drop of blood in the chest cavity. It was as though the arrow had been surgically placed to cause as little damage as possible. If it had entered in any other angle, the projectile would have penetrated the heart's major blood vessels, causing severe bleeding and loss of circulation to the heart muscle. Much more damage and rapid death would have occurred.

I made an incision through the pericardium, the thin sac surrounding the heart that lubricates and protects it. I then created a "pericardial sling" by loosely placing sutures from the pericardium to the sternal retractor. This sling lifted the heart toward me and stabilized it, making it easier to see and manipulate. Now to the important part—how to remove the arrow.

As we already knew, the reason Cupid had survived this injury and had no bleeding from it was that the arrow tip was the same diameter as the shaft. As long as the arrow remained in the heart, the shaft sealed the holes. The heart muscle, especially on the left side, is thick, and it had contracted around the arrow to further tighten the seal. Removing the arrow without closing the holes would result in catastrophic bleeding and immediate death. The dilemma was clear—how could we close the holes while pulling the arrow out?

The answer was "purse string" sutures. Just like it sounds, a purse-string suture is embedded in tissue in a circular pattern so that when it is tied it tightens and closes the opening, whether it be a purse or the heart's muscle.[16] I placed the first suture in the left ventricle surrounding the exposed arrow tip. After notifying the anesthetist of our intentions, we slowly pulled the arrow far enough that the tip was no longer exposed. I started tightening the suture as the arrow tip disappeared into the heart and tied the knot when the hole was closed. Even with the purse-string suture in place, a small jet of blood was pulsing out through the hole. Another suture was quickly placed over the hole, and the bleeding stopped.

Now we turned our attention to the entry point of the arrow in the right ventricle. Again, I placed a purse-string suture, slowly pulled the shaft, and then the entire arrow out while tightening the suture. With the lower blood pressure of the right ventricle compared to the left, there was no bleeding from the hole once the suture was tightened. To be safe, I placed another suture there as well. The arrow was now out of the heart and entirely out of Cupid's chest. We all took a deep breath and watched to see if any bleeding would develop, which thankfully it didn't. We were so grateful to get the arrow out with no complications.

But there were no celebrations yet; we still had work to do. We placed a thoracic drain tube. We took down the pericardial sling, wired the sternum back together, and closed the remaining tissue layers. We moved Cupid to the recovery area and closely monitored her vital signs until she woke up. Then she was placed back into her cage in the ICU for continued treatment and monitoring. One of our concerns after the surgery was the heart's electrical system. The heart has a complicated electrical network that systematically coordinates the muscle contractions. The heart pacemaker, the sinoatrial node, initiates the electrical impulse and regulates the heart rate. Severe heart rate and rhythm disturbances could have occurred if the arrow had injured either the pacemaker or any part of the electrical fibers. Cupid had a few arrhythmias (abnormal beats) on her EKG during surgery, but that is common even in normal dogs under anesthesia. A continuous EKG would be run on Cupid overnight to monitor for any more problems. She would receive antiarrhythmic drugs to prevent abnormal electrical activity. The other treatments for her that night were analgesics (pain-killing drugs) and antibiotics.

Cupid did well overnight and looked good the following day. She was still somewhat sedated and lethargic, but that was no surprise after all she had gone through the day before. Only occasional arrhythmias were seen overnight, and her other vital signs were stable. She looked good for a dog that who had been shot through the heart with an arrow less than twenty-four hours earlier.

The Hole We Could Not See

During my physical examination that morning I discovered a concerning abnormality. Cupid now had a systolic heart murmur—an abnormal swooshing sound in between the "lub" and the "dub" of every heartbeat. Systolic murmurs can occur from various disorders such as leaking heart valves, severe anemia, or a congenital disability. But in Cupid's case, we knew what was causing the murmur. When we removed the arrow, we'd closed the holes in the ventricles. But we did not close the hole in the interventricular septum inside the heart. The leakage of blood between chambers puts more workload on the heart muscle and can lead to heart failure. Fixing this hole would have required open-heart surgery, which we were not prepared to do. Special equipment, like a heart-lung machine and a team of open-heart surgeons and technicians, would have been necessary. Because the septal defect created by the arrow was small, we were hopeful that it would not cause clinical problems and might even heal on its own. We decided to monitor it carefully for the next few weeks.

News about Cupid and her injury not only spread fast in the veterinary hospital, it was big news in the city of Columbus, Ohio as well. Reporters from the local television stations and newspapers came rushing to the clinic to get the story. Part of the reporting was a plea for Cupid's owner to contact the hospital since we still didn't know who they were or where they lived. Her owners saw the story on TV and immediately came to the hospital to see her. They were incredibly relieved that she was all right and doing well. They could not believe that someone would shoot their sweet dog with an arrow. They also told us that her name was Josie. Now we could call her by her real name.

Josie continued to do well and was sent home to her owners three days after surgery. We prescribed an antibiotic to prevent infection, two drugs for pain, and medication to prevent abnormal electrical activity in her heart. We told her owners Josie needed to avoid strenuous exercise. Her heart needed time to heal, and so did the bones of her sternum, which would require several weeks to achieve bony union. Two weeks after the surgery, Josie came back to have her skin stitches removed. She was doing very well at home, not in pain, acting normally, and eating well. Repeat radiographs of her chest showed no abnormalities. Her heart looked normal, and the sternum and wires were intact. But her systolic heart murmur was still present, indicating that the ventricular septal defect made by the arrow had not healed. Josie was discharged with instructions to allow mild exercise after two or three more weeks. We wanted to give her more time to heal and be careful not to put too much workload on her heart until the septum was healed. We suggested she return in a couple of months for a repeat echocardiogram to see how her heart looked.

Three months after the surgery, we saw Josie again at Ohio State. Her owners now wanted to have her spayed, and their regular veterinarian preferred that we do it. I was happy to do it as it would give me a chance to see Josie again and do some more diagnostic tests to see how well her heart was healing. She looked fantastic, like a typical yellow Labrador, energetic, playful, affectionate, and full of life. We did a routine physical examination on her, including listening to her heart. The systolic murmur was gone! An echocardiogram was done and confirmed no leaking of blood across the ventricular septum. The septal hole had healed, and Josie could now live a normal life.

Like most veterinary teaching hospitals at veterinary colleges, at Ohio State, the dogs and cats brought in to be spayed (ovariohysterectomy) or castrated are operated upon and cared for by the fourth-year veterinary students. The students perform the surgery under the supervision of the faculty surgeon or the surgical resident. We watch the students and offer advice, but we don't usually scrub in and assist with the surgery unless necessary. But in Josie's case, given her history, I asked the student if she would mind me assisting her to make sure all went well and wouldn't take too long. She readily accepted my offer. The anesthesia and surgery went well, and no abnormal electrical activity was seen on the EKG during the surgery. Her vital signs were stable during the entire procedure. Josie had survived another operation, which was much less serious than the one three months earlier.

Josie went home the day after the spay. That was the last time I would see her. Over the next several years, I would often wonder how she was doing. My surgery students generated a slide presentation of her to show the other students who were not directly involved in her case. I have shown it to veterinarians worldwide, and they are always amazed at how a dog could live through such an event. I also wrote a blog about Josie (https://drstephenbirchard.blogspot.com/2014/01/the-amazing-story-of-josie-yellow-lab.html), and thus far, over 30,000 people have read her incredible story.

Nine years after the surgery on Josie, I spoke with the original veterinarian who saw her and referred her to Ohio State. He said she was doing well and had no ill effects of her injury. The owners sent me a picture of Josie with their daughter. She looked fantastic.

Over the years, many people, especially children, have asked me, "What is the most amazing patient you've ever operated on?" Until Josie, I had a hard time answering that question. I feel fortunate that I was in the right time and place to be involved in her care. But I also realize that Josie's treatment and recovery resulted from an excellent team effort. The critical care doctors, cardiologists, anesthesiologists, technicians, and students contributed to Josie's state-of-the-art care. I could not have done the surgery without them. Josie was an example of how veterinary medical care can be like what a person would receive in a human hospital.

During my early years on the faculty at Ohio State, the veterinary cardiologists and surgeons developed a collaborative relationship with the "human" cardiologists and cardiac surgeons at the

Ohio State College of Medicine. We worked together in research, teaching laboratories, and on some clinical cases of dogs with congenital disabilities of their heart. The medical school cardiology team even brought their specialized equipment to the veterinary school to help us do open-heart surgery. We learned so much from these cardiac experts, and this experience was invaluable in treating Josie.

But ultimately, it was Josie who had to survive this gruesome injury. And survive she did. She arrived at the hospital wagging her tail with an arrow sticking out of her heart, and after treatment, she left the hospital still wagging her tail. Her biological heart had been injured, but her spiritual heart never missed a beat. It was as though she had a guardian angel looking after her. I believe it was a life-changing experience for all the people involved in her treatment. It certainly was for me. I never would have thought a dog could live through something like that.

The Heart of the Matter

Like the other animals we described in this book, Josie made a miraculous recovery from a life-threatening injury. She was another example of the fantastic ability of the body to withstand trauma and overcome incredible odds to stay alive. One clinical review paper reported that 80-90 percent of people who suffer a gunshot wound to the heart never make it to the hospital. Death usually occurs due to either hemorrhage leading to shock, leakage of blood within the pericardial sac leading to compression of the heart muscle, or heart failure due to damage to the muscle, heart valves, or the electrical conduction system. Josie could easily have suffered any of these complications. I believe forces more significant than all of us worked to save Josie and allowed her to live on for many years to be a loving companion to her family and others. In the last picture I have of her, some nine years after the injury, the owner's daughter is hugging Josie around her neck, and she is smiling from ear to ear. The mutual love between them shines through the picture. It provides the compelling reason why this adorable yellow Labrador retriever was meant to live.

Courage Is Not the Absence of Fear . . .

". . . but rather the assessment that something else is more important than fear." (Franklin D. Roosevelt) In other words, courage is the ability to act despite fear.

If I am candid about why my hands were trembling as we started the surgery, it's because I was scared. The heart is particularly difficult to work on since the constant beating makes it a moving target. A wrong decision or technical error could lead to a catastrophe. I had to somehow work through this fear for the sake of my patient. The confidence others had in me bolstered my courage and helped me stay calm and collected. Although it was a surgery I had not done or seen before, I knew what we had to do and used the principles I had been taught to remove the arrow. You could say that everything I had learned up to that point had prepared me for what was necessary for Josie. Josie showed me that I could overcome my fear of making a mistake and perform a surgery I had never done before. She gave me an opportunity to grow as a professional. That is why Josie is the most memorable patient I have ever treated.

Have you ever been in a situation where you had to do something necessary but were paralyzed by fear? Maybe Josie's story can be a source of inspiration for you the next time you face what appears to be an impossible task. You may find that you will dare to do what must be done, especially if you prepare yourself for the job. By going outside your "comfort zone," you expand that zone. You begin to feel more confident, confronting your fears and experiencing personal growth and satisfaction. All because of a mild-mannered yellow Labrador who didn't give up, even after getting shot through the heart.

Chapter 5: Billy Bob

W hen veterinary schools or specialty
practices become temporarily short-
handed, they invite specialists from
other hospitals to fill in, like a substitute teacher. I've
been asked to do a number of these over the years
but usually declined them. I was either too busy or
didn't want to adapt to a different hospital with

unknown people, facilities, and equipment. But several years ago, when the Kansas State University College of Veterinary Medicine called and asked me to be a visiting clinician for a week, I immediately accepted. I had some old friends there, including the dean, Dr. Ralph Richardson, the hospital director, Dr. Roger Fingland (my first surgery resident at Ohio State), and Dr. Dave Biller, head of the radiology department. I was interested in experiencing the workings of their hospital and seeing some old friends in the process. It was at the Kansas State vet school that I met Billy Bob.

My first day at K State started with getting to know everyone on my service—the chief surgery resident, the intern, and the students. Honestly, I was a little nervous about being there. I didn't know my way around. The students and residents were unfamiliar, and I didn't know much about the facility. But I just tried to stay loose and let the experience come to me. Little did I know I would meet one of the most memorable patients and owners of my entire career.

My group consisted of three fourth-year veterinary students and a surgical resident. In his third year of the surgical training program, the resident was well versed in the workings of the clinic and its daily activities. We all introduced ourselves and spent a little time getting to know each other and getting me oriented.

We started by doing rounds to look at our in-patients from the weekend. All the hospitalized dogs and cats were stable and doing well. Then it was time to start seeing new patient appointments in the clinic. My first patient was Billy Bob. I read her previous medical record to become familiar with her before meeting her and the owner in person.

Love at First Sight

Billy Bob was a six-year-old spayed female boxer who was in excellent physical condition and just as energetic and lovable as she could be. As I walked into the examination room with her, she jumped on my lap, licked my face, and slobbered her affection all over me. I was covered with Billy Bob's hair and saliva within a few minutes. I immediately fell in love with her.

When Billy let me come up for air, I introduced myself to Bruce, her owner. We immediately hit it off. A middle-aged, successful hotel owner, he was very down-to-earth, polite, and warm-hearted. He obviously loved Billy Bob. Not just a pet, Billy was also his service dog. Bruce had diabetes, and Billy was trained to monitor him for low blood sugar. Dogs can detect changes in blood sugar by smelling their owner's breath or sweat.[17] Although not as sensitive as continuous blood sugar monitoring devices, dogs can provide many benefits to diabetic patients. When his blood sugar dropped, Billy would alert Bruce by jumping on him and licking his face.

In this way, Bruce could do whatever was necessary to get his blood sugar back up before he might pass out and potentially hurt himself. Bruce traveled a lot with his work, and Billy always went with him. I've seen this kind of intimate relationship between dog and owner many times over the years, but this bond was exceptional, and I knew that it meant Bruce was willing to do whatever was necessary for Billy.

On my initial examination of Billy Bob, she did not look sick at all. She appeared very healthy, strong, and energetic. But there was a problem brewing inside her. She had started bleeding from her nose about a year earlier. Bruce had been traveling for work with Billy as his usual close companion, even on airplanes. On one of their trips, as they went through airport security, the TSA agent pulled Bruce aside and told him he saw some blood coming from Billy's nose. As soon as he returned from the trip, Bruce took Billy to his veterinarian, who referred them to the veterinary hospital at Kansas State for more diagnostics.

At K State, they performed a CAT scan of her nose and nasal cavity. A tumor in her nasal cavity was found on the scan, and a biopsy of the lesion showed cancer. It was a malignancy of the cartilage inside her nose, called chondrosarcoma. Although cancerous, this type of tumor is not as bad as some others that dogs can get in that part of their body. But it's still cancer; curing it was not likely. Billy Bob with cancer was not the news Bruce wanted to hear about his cherished friend.

After the initial diagnosis, the K State team treated Billy Bob with radiation therapy of her entire nasal cavity. Radiation therapy is a potent anti-cancer weapon that involves up to twenty daily treatments. Each treatment requires general anesthesia to prevent patient movement and allow accurate focusing of the radiation beam. Complications are common, such as skin inflammation, pain, and damage to the eyes. Luckily, Billy suffered only minor issues associated with the therapy and sailed through the treatments like a champ. She did well for about six months. Then the nasal bleeding returned, and a second CAT scan showed that cancer in her nose had come back. That's when I entered the picture.

On my examination of Billy, her nose and face looked fine other than a small amount of nasal discharge. The rest of the physical examination of Billy was normal. She was a beautiful, stately boxer dog with a fabulous personality and a heart as big as Kansas.

I sat down with Bruce to discuss our plan and explain the risks of surgery to remove Billy's tumor and the expected outcome. The radiation therapy had been done from the top of her nose. Although unconventional, I recommended a ventral surgical approach to her nasal cavity through the hard palate in her mouth (also called a ventral rhinotomy). The usual way to open the nasal cavity in a dog is to go from the top of her nose through the nasal bone. But I was concerned that the radiation had damaged those tissues and reduced their capacity for healing. The tumor did not appear very large on the CAT scan, and I felt I could get it out through this alternative approach. But I told Bruce honestly that I didn't expect the surgery to cure Billy's cancer. Surgery would remove most of the tumor, but any that remained would have to be treated either with more radiation or chemotherapy.

I was concerned that removing some of her nasal tissues would diminish her ability to smell. Research has shown that dogs use their sense of smell for much more than we imagined.[17] Not only can they sense low blood sugar, but dogs can also be trained to detect cancer in people using their incredible sense of smell. If Billy's sense of smell was essential to managing Bruce's diabetes, nasal surgery could diminish that capability.

I was concerned about how Bruce would take this information, especially considering he didn't know me. I wasn't a permanent faculty member at K-State. I planned to do a major operation on his beloved companion and do it in an unconventional way. There would be some blood loss and potential problems with the healing of the surgical site even though we were avoiding the radiated area. Some owner anxiety and apprehension about the situation would have been perfectly normal. But the K State staff assured Bruce that I was qualified to perform the surgery. He had investigated other possible hospitals to take Billy but decided that K State was the best option. I'm sure glad he did. I was honored that Bruce trusted me to operate on Billy. That feeling of trust and shared commitment between owner and veterinarian is an essential part of the relationship. I was glad we were off to such a good start. It was a friendship that would grow stronger over the months and years to come.

Billy Bob was admitted to the hospital. Routine blood tests and chest radiographs were obtained to ensure she was suitable for anesthesia and surgery. They all checked out well. The next day Billy was placed under general anesthesia and prepared for the surgery. Billy was placed on her back in the operating room with her head at the end of the table. We put an oral speculum in her mouth to keep it open, rinsed her mouth with an oral antiseptic, and draped her in. We made a large incision in the roof of her mouth through the mucosa (gums) of her hard palate. We then exposed the bone of her hard palate. We used an oscillating bone saw to remove a rectangular section of the bone to expose the inside of her nasal cavity.

We saw the cancer immediately, mostly on the left side of her nasal cavity. It was shaped like the florets of a cauliflower, very soft and easily fragmented, and tannish yellow. The tumor was buried between the nasal turbinates. The turbinates are an intricate labyrinth of eggshell thin bones

111

covered with delicate membranes. They are part of the reason dogs have such an incredible sense of smell. The turbinates have a rich blood supply—if you've ever had a nosebleed you'd understand. To remove Billy's tumor, we had to remove some of these turbinates and part of the nasal septum, all of which caused severe bleeding. We worked quickly and used suction to see the tissues. I removed the tumor and promptly packed the nasal cavity with Nugauze, a ribbon-like gauze material that soaks up the blood and allows it to clot to help arrest further bleeding. The packing would stay in for a couple of days and then be removed. We closed the incision and moved Billy out of the surgical suite and into the anesthesia recovery area.

Billy Bob recovered well from anesthesia and was taken to the intensive care unit. K State has a beautiful, spacious intensive care unit for small animals. Billy Bob was placed in a comfortable cage where the nurses could watch her overnight. We wrote up her treatment orders and got her settled in for what we hoped would be an uneventful night. I called Bruce and let him know how things went. I was pleased with the surgery; I felt we had removed the entire visible tumor. There were no unexpected complications during the procedure. Although Billy had lost some blood, her postoperative blood tests showed only a minor decrease in her red blood cell count, so a transfusion was unnecessary. Bruce was happy with the positive report, and I promised we would update him in the morning.

Billy had a good night, resting comfortably with minimal bleeding from her nose. The following day, she was somewhat quiet and not her usual rambunctious self, probably because of the potent narcotic pain relievers we were giving her. But she looked good, considering the major operation she'd just had. She even ate a little breakfast, and her bodily functions were in good working order. The student assigned to Billy's care called Bruce with the excellent report. Billy did fine the remainder of the day and even ate a full meal in the afternoon.

On day two after surgery, Billy continued to do well. She was bright, alert, eating, and readily accepting our requests for affection. We pulled the nasal packing from Billy's nose that afternoon. She sneezed a few times immediately afterward and had slight bleeding from her nose, but it quickly stopped, and all was fine. I felt it best to keep Billy hospitalized one more day to prevent nasal bleeding.

We sent Billy home with Bruce the next day. She looked great, and Bruce was very pleased. One advantage of the oral approach to the nasal cavity is that you couldn't see any evidence that surgery had been done unless you looked inside Billy's mouth. We told Bruce to feed her soft food and flush her mouth with water after eating, avoid letting her chew any hard or rough toys or bones, and let her rest for several days while she recovered.

I was a little sad to see her go—her limitless affection and playful attitude were infectious, and I loved being with her. Billy certainly didn't seem to hold any grudges with me for having put her through a major operation on her mouth and nose. She quickly got past all that and was still very generous doling out the face licks. I hoped she would continue to do well at home.

A few days after Billy went home, my week at K State ended. Before I left, I told the chief resident to be sure to let me know how Billy was doing when she came back in for her postoperative recheck. I wanted to be sure her incision was healing well and that there was no nasal discharge. Bruce did bring her back on schedule, and all was going well. She was healing beautifully, her nose was clean with just a little clear discharge but no blood, and she was eating well and acting very normal. Additional rechecks with the medical oncologist were scheduled to determine what other therapy would be considered to prevent recurrence of the cancer.

Some weeks later, after her mouth was completely healed, Billy went back to K State for a second round of radiation therapy on her nose. The goal was to eliminate any remaining cancer cells. She again came through this well with minimal complications.

The Cancer Was Down, But Not Out

Billy did very well for several months after this second radiation treatment. She was acting normally, eating well, and enjoying life as a dog. About nine months after her surgery, the bloody nasal discharge returned. Fearing cancer recurrence, Bruce immediately took her to Kansas State for a recheck examination. A repeat CT scan showed that the nasal chondrosarcoma was back. It didn't appear to be as big as last time, but it was there, nonetheless. This was a setback, and everyone was disappointed. We'd known it was unlikely to cure the cancer, but after two rounds of radiation therapy combined with surgical removal of the tumor, we didn't expect it to re-grow so quickly.

Bruce called me as soon as the CT scan results were available. Since treating Billy at K State, I retired from my faculty position at Ohio State. I was now doing part-time clinical work at a specialty practice in Minneapolis. I told Bruce to send me the CT images, and I would evaluate them and make a recommendation. Although smaller than the tumor we had seen in January, there was re-growth of cancer in the exact location as the one I had removed only nine months earlier. Bruce told me that Billy Bob was doing well otherwise, eating, active, and as playful as usual.

I told Bruce I would recommend operating again to remove the recurrent tumor. I thought it was the best option as the CT scan showed a visible tumor, and since Billy did so well with the first surgery she should do just as well the second time around. After surgery, if the radiation oncology doctors thought it was feasible, they could irradiate the nasal cavity again to control any remaining microscopic tumor. Without hesitation, Bruce agreed and said he would immediately drive Billy to Minneapolis so I could do the surgery. I said it would be fine for the surgeons at K State to do the surgery since it would be such a long drive from Kansas to Minnesota. But he insisted that since Billy was my patient, he wanted me to do it. I didn't fight him too hard on his decision—I wanted to see Billy again and spend time with her and Bruce.

A couple of days later, Bruce and Billy showed up at the practice. He had a large recreational vehicle that he used for his cross-country trips, and he drove it from Kansas City to Minneapolis with Billy as his co-pilot. The RV gave Billy Bob lots of space to roam around during the long journeys—only the best for his cherished companion.

Billy looked great as usual; she was energetic, happy, and jumped into my lap as soon as she saw me. Other than a trace of nasal discharge, you would not have had any idea this dog was living with cancer. Her attitude was as cheerful as ever. I sometimes think that sick animals have an advantage over humans; they embody "ignorance is bliss." By not knowing anything about their illness, they don't let it get them down. They don't wonder how long they will live or how much they will suffer. They charge ahead as if everything's fine, living entirely in the present and enjoying whatever comes their way. Our "higher intelligence" can be our downfall in times of severe illness or injury. This is just one of many things we can learn from our four-legged friends.

I did not have to discuss the surgery very much with Bruce. He and Billy had been through this before, and I planned to do the procedure exactly as we had done it the first time. Billy's nose had been irradiated twice in two years, and I wasn't about to traumatize the fragile tissue with a dorsal approach (through the top of the nose). We planned to approach the nasal cavity through the mouth again. Less bone would need to be removed this time, so the surgery would be shorter in duration.

The day after she arrived at the clinic, we got Billy ready for surgery. Her preoperative blood tests and radiographs looked good. Before beginning the anesthesia, she looked up at me with her trusting eyes, and I told her I would do all I could to get the cancer out of her. She didn't understand the words, but I think she felt my optimism. She wasn't giving up, and neither was I.

With her under anesthesia and positioned for the surgery, I made an incision on Billy's hard palate in the exact place we had nine months ago. The bony defect was still present, although some thick scar tissue had formed in the space where we removed the bone. I entered the nasal cavity, and the tumor was apparent; however, this time it looked different. It was softer and more diffuse, not as well-formed, with the consistency of cottage cheese. I removed as much as possible, mainly by scooping it out with curettes, forceps, and suction. There was some bleeding but not as much as with the first surgery. Many of the turbinates had already been removed, so there was just scar tissue adjacent to the tumor. We packed the nasal cavity again, but this time with a product called Vetspon, a spongy material that looks like Styrofoam. It is made of gelatin and helps stop bleeding by providing the framework for a clot to form. Over time it is entirely absorbed by the body, so there would be no need to remove the gauze packing as we had with the first surgery.

Billy recovered well from anesthesia, and we got her bedded down in the ICU. We wrote her treatment orders, and I kept an eye on her myself between my remaining surgeries. Bruce had been hanging out in his RV the whole time, so I went out to the parking lot after the surgery to see him and let him know that all was well. I told him the cancer had been more diffuse and harder to remove this time. But Billy was doing well, and I expected her to make a good recovery like she had before. We sent all the removed tissues off for analysis by the pathologist.

Of course, the morning after surgery, when I got to the hospital and went to Billy's cage, she jumped up, wagged her tail, and ran out to me as if nothing had happened. What a fantastic creature to bounce back so quickly from both aggressive surgeries on her nose. She looked fantastic. Bruce came to visit her, and my only concern was that she would be so active she might start bleeding from the nose. Luckily, she continued to do well that first postoperative day.

I had Dr. Brian Husbands, the veterinary oncologist at the clinic, consult on Billy's case to see what else we should do to treat her cancer. He felt that chemotherapy would not be effective for this cancer since it was chondrosarcoma. Another round of radiation therapy could be considered. Although not curative, at least radiation could give her more time until the tumor grew back.

Bruce and I had a long talk about Billy's future treatment and prognosis. She had already lived longer than most dogs with this type of cancer. Her resilient attitude, excellent physical condition, and Bruce's commitment to her had led to good results so far. But Bruce understood that although we were helping Billy with surgery and radiation therapy, we were not curing her cancer. At some point, it would probably rear its ugly head again. Unfortunately, there would be more cancer in Billy's future, but not how we expected.

On day two after surgery, Billy continued to do well. After taking a few pictures of Billy with Bruce, my wife Becky, and our six-month-old son Stuart, Bruce loaded her up in the RV and headed back to

Kansas. I told him to keep us updated on her progress and that I would send a full report back to K State for their records. The RV pulled away as Billy watched us out the window with tail wagging. I wondered to myself when and how I would see her again.

As promised, Bruce kept me updated. Every few months I would get a call or text to let me know that Billy was doing fine, with no nasal discharge, no sneezing, and a normal appetite. He sent frequent pictures of Billy in the RV, at home, or on his farm. Even one year after the second surgery, there were no signs of cancer recurrence.

Was it possible we had finally beat this tumor? It seemed unlikely given the nature of this cancer, but one can always hope. I was at least glad that Bruce was getting lots of quality time with his companion and that she was continuing to provide the medical service he needed.

A Third Surgery, in a Third City

Billy's cancer eventually returned but in a different part of her body. Fourteen months after her second surgery, she developed swelling of her lower jaw. A CT scan showed that something was eating away the jawbones (mandibles). A jaw biopsy confirmed that it was cancer, although it wasn't immediately clear if it was the same cancer as in her nose.

Bruce called me with the bad news. I had moved again and was working in a specialty practice in Indianapolis. This, of course, was not a problem for Bruce; he was already packing to bring Billy to me for another surgery. Finding a tumor in Billy's jaw was another setback, but Bruce and I weren't ready to give up, and neither was Billy.

A couple of days later, Bruce and Billy arrived at Indianapolis. We admitted her to the hospital and got her ready for the surgery. It would be another big operation for Billy. We would have to remove the front part of her lower jaw to remove the tumor. The surgery is called a rostral mandibulectomy. The chin would then need to be reconstructed and attached to the cut ends of her jawbones. Surprisingly, most dogs do very well with this kind of surgery. I had performed the surgery many times on other dogs and was comfortable with the procedure. But I didn't like having to subject Billy to yet another major operation.

We placed Billy under anesthesia, clipped and scrubbed her chin and cheeks for surgery, placed her on the operating table, and draped her in. We removed the soft tissues from the bone near the tumor. Then we cut the mandibles with an oscillating bone saw like what we had used for her nasal surgeries. We had to remove about 40 percent of her lower jaw. After controlling bleeding, the gums and skin of the chin were sutured back to cover the bone. To secure the chin on the bone, I placed large sutures through holes drilled in the ends of the mandibles, then brought the suture through the chin. Surgical buttons were used on her chin to cushion the sutures and keep them from pulling through the skin. It went very well, and as usual, Billy made an excellent recovery from the anesthesia and surgery. We moved her to the ICU and wrote up her treatment orders. After mandibulectomy, an essential part of treatment is pain control. Billy was kept on intravenous fentanyl overnight.

The following day, Billy looked excellent, much better than I expected. There was some mild swelling of her chin but minimal bleeding overnight. She was comfortable, and she even ate breakfast! Imagine, if you will, having that kind of surgery on yourself and then eating breakfast within twenty-four hours. Billy was indeed a resilient dog and a fantastic patient. I gave Bruce the good news on her recovery. He couldn't wait to visit her.

We kept Billy in the hospital one more day then sent her home with Bruce. I told him to keep us updated. The surgeons at K State would remove her chin buttons two weeks later. I sent the jaw tumor off to the pathology lab to find out what type of cancer it was and forwarded those results to the K State and Bruce. Yet again, I was sorry to see Billy go. I didn't know it then, but it would be the last time I would see her.

Analysis of the tumor showed that it was the same type as in her nose, chondrosarcoma. The other bad news was that the cancer was invasive. Even with the mandibulectomy, there were still cancer cells in her mouth. It was probably an extension of the nasal tumor. I forwarded the findings to the oncologist at K State and Bruce, who asked what else should be done for Billy at this point. I told him I would consult with the K State cancer specialists and see what they thought could be done. More radiation was an option, but she had already been through so many treatments we weren't sure if it was possible. The K-State doctors would discuss this with Bruce when he brought Billy in for her postop recheck and button removal.

She Won the Battles but Lost the War

Bruce brought Billy in for her recheck exam at K State about sixteen days after her mandibulectomy. She was doing all right—her jaw had healed well and the chin buttons were removed. But she seemed to be uncomfortable in her rear legs. On her physical exam, she was painful in her hind legs, pelvis, and abdomen. A CT scan was performed the next day and showed that her cancer had spread. Her spinal canal, kidneys, liver, lymph nodes, and lungs had tumors. Biopsies were done and confirmed that the chondrosarcoma had spread throughout her body. Suddenly and with no warning, Billy was losing the battle with her cancer.

As soon as I heard the news, I called Bruce, and of course, he was devastated. The outlook for Billy now was poor—very little could be done for her other than making her comfortable with pain-relieving medication. Bruce wasn't ready to euthanize Billy, but he understood that it would need to be considered soon. His loyal friend, companion, and service dog was dying.

On February 17, 2014, Bruce's birthday, he had Billy euthanized. Even potent analgesic medication could not control her pain, and she had rapidly deteriorated. Putting her to sleep was the most difficult decision he had ever made, but it had to be done to be fair to his friend and relieve her suffering. He buried her on his farm in Kansas. On her grave is a beautiful gravestone with her picture on it. She had lived for eight years and four months and had dedicated her entire life to serving Bruce.

Bruce owns many hotels all over the country. He dedicated one of them to Billy Bob, in a gesture to recognize all she had done for him. Bruce and I have talked many times since Billy died. He cannot emphasize enough what Billy meant to him. Their bond was much more than that of a typical owner and pet. She was a vital part of his life, not just for the medical service she provided but also for the emotional and spiritual support she gave him. Bruce was a Vietnam veteran and had been exposed to Agent Orange during that war. Severe health effects are common after that exposure, and he told me his diabetes was at least partly due to that toxin in his body. Billy helped him deal with the physical and mental stresses resulting from his experience in Vietnam.

Billy went through a war of her own. In the three years after being diagnosed with cancer, she had three major surgeries and three courses of radiation therapy that each lasted three to four weeks. She had taken countless trips to the Kansas State Veterinary Hospital and traveled to three different cities for her surgeries. Through all her trials and tribulations, she never lost her affection, strength, or vitality until the very end. Clinical studies have shown that with treatment, the usual survival in dogs with nasal chondrosarcoma is one to two years.[18] Billy easily beat those numbers. She was indeed an amazing animal, and her story offers some hope to others fighting the battle against cancer.

I believe that three factors contributed to Billy's prolonged survival: her medical treatment, purpose, and support system. The medical treatment, the combination of surgery and radiation therapy, was the best we could offer for an animal like Billy or even a person with the same illness. There is plenty of evidence-based medicine to show that the treatment Billy received provides the best chance of prolonging life with chondrosarcoma of the nasal cavity.

A Purpose-driven Life

But just as important as the medical factor in Billy's success were her life's purpose and the love and affection surrounding her. Bruce had Billy trained to provide an essential service for him. He sent her to a facility in Colorado to receive this advanced training and skill. Billy spent the rest of her life helping Bruce and preventing him from experiencing catastrophic decreases in blood sugar. Her service to Bruce gave Billy a mission that she would maintain until she passed away. Dogs love to have a job, and Billy's not only kept Bruce alive; it kept her alive as well.

Finally, Billy Bob was surrounded by a family, especially a man, who loved her dearly. He showed his affection for her openly and without hesitation. Love is the most potent medicine, and Billy got a hefty dose of it her entire life.

Bruce and Billy Bob didn't realize it at the time, but allowing me to join them in Billy's battle against cancer helped me personally. The three years that I knew Billy and Bruce were some of the most tumultuous years of my life. After retiring from my faculty position at Ohio State, I moved three times, got divorced, remarried, had a baby, and experienced a devastating loss when my mom died unexpectedly. Bonding with Bruce and Billy comforted me in a time of instability, grief, and new beginnings. They followed me to three different cities to operate on Billy's cancer. Knowing how much Bruce loved Billy, the trust he placed in me was almost overwhelming. He validated my knowledge and abilities, and it meant the world to me. I remember so many long conversations, often in the evening, when Bruce and I would talk about Billy and how much she meant to him. Although I only knew her in the last phase of her life, she also meant a lot to me, as did my friendship with Bruce. After her death, he told me that I was now a permanent part of his family. Thank you for that, Bruce; I am honored by your trust and friendship. May Billy Bob rest in peace. If dogs go to heaven (and I think they do), she is there wagging her tail, jumping on laps, and affectionately slobbering on everyone she meets.

Chapter 6: Jack

As they walked out of the University of Minnesota Veterinary Hospital, his owners were still trying to process the news they had just received. Jack, their handsome golden retriever, had cancer. The doctors told them that surgery was not an option, and chemotherapy would not be effective. Radiation treatments could be tried, but the tumor would likely grow back and eventually spread to other parts of his body. He didn't have long to live, and he was only four years old.

His owners were devastated. Their heads swirled with questions: What had caused it, why did he have cancer at such a young age, what should they do next? They were very worried about their lovable, loyal companion.

Jack's owners had gotten him as a puppy from a "backyard breeder," someone who breeds dogs more as a hobby than a business. They fell in love with him from day one. He loved people—he never met a person he didn't like. Several months after getting Jack, his owners brought an English cocker spaniel into the home. Whenever a second dog is introduced into a family, there's a risk that the canine roommates will not exactly appreciate one another's company. The first dog of the house, the one with "seniority," may become jealous and a bit grouchy with the new intruder. Not so with Jack—he loved the cocker pup right from the beginning. He played with him, was very gentle, and showed no signs of annoyance or jealousy. He accepted his new friend into his life with no reservations.

Jack lived his first several years with no health problems, making regular visits to his vet and getting vaccinated against all the common diseases. He was sound in mind and body. Unfortunately, that all abruptly changed.

Jack began making strange noises from his nose and mouth, sort of like snoring, but he made the sounds when he was awake, not sleeping. His owners were concerned by the noises and took him to see their local veterinarian. After finding a tumor in his throat, the vet referred them to the University of Minnesota vet school. Once they had a chance to process the bad news from the specialists at the university, Jack's owners decided to get a second opinion.

Jack came to the Blue Pearl Veterinary Specialty Clinic in Eden Prairie, Minnesota, and was examined by my wife, Dr. Becky Ball. Like me, she specializes in veterinary surgery. She recommended that Jack be sedated so that she could get a good look at the mass and obtain a biopsy. The biopsy would give her a definitive diagnosis of the tumor—the exact tumor type and what tissue it came from. With that information, she could make treatment recommendations.

Becky sedated Jack and then examined the tumor. It was huge, and in a bad location. It was round, about four centimeter in diameter, and was located at the back of the roof of his mouth. It was easy to see why he was making noise during breathing. It was amazing he could breathe at all with this gigantic mass in his mouth. The tumor was hard, most likely coming from the bone of the hard palate. It extended from his molar teeth on one side to the molar teeth on the other side of his mouth. The size and location of the tumor are why doctors at the University of Minnesota did not think surgery was feasible.

Becky obtained a biopsy of the mass with a biopsy punch device. The procedure went well, and Jack recovered quickly from anesthesia and went home that evening. When Becky got home that night, she showed me pictures of the tumor and asked my opinion. I said we needed to wait for the biopsy results, but if the tumor was not highly malignant and if there was no evidence it had spread to other body parts, we might be able to remove it surgically. It would require a bilateral partial maxillectomy, an aggressive surgical procedure involving the removal of a large section of the hard palate and tissue from the nasal cavity. I had performed the surgery on several other dogs, but it was technically challenging and associated with serious risks such as blood loss and poor healing of the tissues. Jack's owners would need to be educated on the surgery and potential complications.

A few days later, some good news came in. Jack's chest radiographs showed no spreading of the cancer, and a fine needle aspirate biopsy of the lymph nodes in his neck also showed no cancer. The pathology report on the mass biopsy revealed a multilobulated osteochondrosarcoma, abbreviated as MLO. This tumor is considered cancerous, but it is not as bad as other tumors in the mouth, such as osteosarcoma or melanoma. If we could achieve a complete resection of the cancer, Jack could live for several more years. But removing the entire tumor would be very challenging.

To better prepare us for the surgery, we sent Jack back to the University of Minnesota for a CT scan of his mouth and head. This imaging would tell us how much of the hard palate bone had been invaded by the tumor and if it extended into the maxillary bones and nasal cavity. This information would help us plan the surgery and determine how much bone and soft tissue to remove. The CT scan showed invasion of the bone of the hard palate, but the tumor did not extend beyond the level of the molar teeth on either side. So although the surgery would be extensive, we might be able to get the entire tumor out.

Becky called the owners with this news. They were excited to hear that there was at least a chance that we could remove the tumor and that if successful, Jack could have many more years of life ahead of him. But she also warned them of potential blood loss that could require a blood transfusion, poor healing of the tissues of the mouth necessitating multiple surgeries, and postoperative pain and difficulty eating until the mouth was healed. A feeding tube might have to be placed to avoid food getting stuck in his mouth and causing more problems with healing and infection.

Jack's owners didn't need much time to consider what course of action to take. They loved their dog and wanted to do whatever they could to help him beat the cancer in his mouth. Although the treatment might be difficult and his recovery prolonged, surgery was his best chance. They scheduled the surgery for just a few days after the CT scan. In the meantime, Becky and I began preparing ourselves for what would be a complicated surgical procedure.

We reviewed the relevant anatomy of the area. Good surgeons have tremendous respect for anatomy since it's essential to know where all vital structures are located and avoid causing unnecessary damage to the animal. The oral cavity is a part of the body with a rich network of arteries and veins supplying the mouth and throat tissues with blood. This is an advantage since a good blood supply helps the mouth heal and reduces infection. But from a surgical standpoint, it also meant that, even if we were careful to avoid cutting large blood vessels, there would be profuse bleeding during the surgery. Bleeding would make the operation difficult and could be dangerous for Jack. Blood transfusions, although rarely needed, could be necessary if it became excessive.

Another aspect of the surgery that we needed to prepare for was the reconstruction of Jack's mouth after tumor removal. We would be removing a considerable section of the roof of his mouth, which would leave a defect extending into his nasal cavity. Excising the tumor would be challenging enough; fixing the gaping hole in his hard palate would be even more daunting. The reconstruction would be like closing a severe cleft palate. We reviewed all the options and came up with a game plan.

En Bloc Excision

A few days later, Jack was admitted to the hospital for his surgery. As usual, he was in good spirits, but his owners were anxious. They knew Jack was facing a major operation and that complications were common. Since we would be performing the surgery later in the afternoon, the owners went home to await our call after it was completed.

Jack was placed under general anesthesia; his mouth was cleaned and prepared for the surgery. We don't consider this a sterile operation. But we still clean the mouth as much as possible and use sterile equipment to prevent infection. Jack also received intravenous antibiotics during the procedure.

He was laid on his back, his mouth held open with an oral speculum. Becky was Jack's attending clinician, so she was the primary surgeon. I assisted her. She used a sterile marking pen to draw lines around the mass to indicate where we would make our incisions. We would be removing not just the tumor but everything the tumor was attached to— the oral mucosa, some of the teeth, the bone of the hard palate, and some of the nasal tissue. Removing the mass and all adjacent tissue as a complete section is called en bloc excision. In this way, we had the best chance of completely removing the tumor.

Using a scalpel, Becky made the initial incisions around the tumor. The bleeding began in earnest, making it difficult to see the deeper tissues. We used electrocautery to control the bleeding and suction to clear the surgical site of blood and fluid. Once we dissected the soft tissue off the bone around the mass, Becky made cuts in the bone of the hard palate using an air-driven bone burr, like what dentists use when they prepare teeth for a filling. These cuts with the burr were done entirely around the tumor and then finished with an osteotome (a surgical chisel). After the bone holding the cancer was completely cut, we carefully removed the section of bone, gum tissue, and tumor from the mouth. Some nasal turbinates were gently removed like the surgery in Billy Bob in Chapter 5. This caused more bleeding, so we packed the nasal cavity with gauze, which helped control the hemorrhage.

After removing the giant tumor and attached bone, we did more bleeding control and flushed the area with sterile saline. For a minute or two, we stared at the size of the massive hole in Jack's mouth and wondered if our plan to reconstruct it would work. Before closing the defect, we packed Jack's nasal cavity with Vetspon to control the bleeding.

To close the defect in Jack's hard palate, Becky made rectangular flaps of the gum tissue inside of each of Jack's upper lips and stretched them across the defect. One was made on each side, advanced toward the middle of the hole, and sutured to each other. We carefully lifted each flap from the underlying tissue. If not done correctly, the flaps would lose their blood supply, and the tissue would die. The reconstruction plan worked, but only time would tell if the flaps would hold over the next several days.

After the surgery, Jack was moved to the recovery area to wake up from anesthesia, then finally placed in his cage in the ICU. He was given very potent pain relievers including intravenous fentanyl. Jack needed potent analgesic drugs since he had just experienced an extensive and painful surgical procedure. Imagine pain many times worse than having your wisdom teeth removed.

The next day Jack was weak, and his muzzle was swollen, but he seemed comfortable and even ate a small breakfast. He had some bleeding from his nose and frequently snorted and sneezed when his mouth was closed. He occasionally tried to paw at his face, indicating that his mouth hurt. We began to use ice packs on his nose to reduce swelling and pain. He needed some sedation to tolerate the cold packs.

Two days after surgery, Jack had continued to improve and even looked good enough to be discharged from the hospital. His face was still swollen, and he was making noise when breathing with his mouth closed, but he was eating well and seemed comfortable. The owners were delighted to bring him back home, and Becky explained what to expect and how to care for him. He went home on three different pain medications: Carprofen (a non-steroidal anti-inflammatory), Tramadol, a synthetic opioid, and a fentanyl transdermal patch.

Instructions were to feed Jack canned food made into meatballs to make it easier to chew and swallow and monitor his breathing and general attitude and activity. He was not allowed to chew on bones or other hard toys to prevent damage to the incisions in his mouth. We reminded his owners that complications were common after this surgery, and the mucosal flaps could break down at any time. One sign of this happening would be a foul odor from Jack's mouth and food and water coming out of his nose. We told his owners to immediately bring him back to the clinic if they developed.

Surgical Principle: Don't Suture Tissues Under Tension

It didn't take long for problems to arise. Soon after Jack went home, the owners became concerned that he wasn't drinking any water. They were afraid that he could become dehydrated, so they brought him back through the emergency service for fluid therapy. That seemed to make him feel better, and he was treated as an outpatient and sent back home.

Then more serious problems arose. After being home for only two days, Jack became lethargic and stopped eating, and a foul odor emanated from his mouth. The owners brought him back to the hospital, and Jack was admitted. We looked inside his mouth and saw some breakdown of the flap incisions. They were not healing, and the stitches could not hold the flaps together. There was too much tension across the suture line. Although we had warned Jack's owners about this possibility, it happened sooner than expected. We began treating Jack with antibiotics to combat infection in his mouth.

When an incision like this begins to fall apart, the temptation is to try to re-suture the torn mucous membranes immediately. But for the first several days after surgery, the tissues are at their peak of inflammation, thickened, easily torn, and not strong enough to hold sutures. Re-suturing would have to wait several days until the inflammation calmed down and the tissues strengthened. A reasonable plan, but it created another problem. As the flap incisions opened, it left a hole that led directly into the nasal cavity. Now food and water could get up into his nose, causing infection and nasal discharge. To prevent this, Jack's owners would have to very carefully and slowly feed him canned dog food made into small meatballs so he could easily chew and swallow the food without it going through the hole in the roof of his mouth. Then they would need to gently flush his mouth with water to clean out any remaining food that might be stuck in there.

Jack's owners were dedicated and highly conscientious people. They did everything we recommended, and Jack quickly began to feel better.

He ate the meatballs well and tolerated the mouth flushing. The odor from his mouth improved.

When this healing complication was occurring, some good news came in. The pathologist who analyzed the tissue samples that we submitted from his mouth felt confident that we had achieved clean margins. In other words, we had removed the entire tumor, and there was no microscopic evidence of any cancer remaining. This was great news and meant he could have a good outcome from the surgery, and the cancer was unlikely to grow back. We just needed to get his mouth to heal!

Over the next several days, Jack continued to improve, and he began to behave like his usual self. He seemed comfortable and was eating with no difficulty and no discharge from his nose. He presented to Becky about four days after the flap broke down so she could re-examine his mouth and see how things looked. There were two areas where the flap incision had opened, and both openings communicated with the nasal cavity. Repair of these areas would not be easy. There was very little tissue to work with, so it would not be a simple case of re-stitching the incisions. We would have to figure out how to fill the defects with something other than his gum tissue.

Lend Me Your Ear (Or Just Part of It)

As Becky usually does, she researched clinical veterinary articles for ideas to fix Jack's mouth. The veterinary dentist working with us in the clinic, Dr. Donnell Hansen, told us she had recently read some case reports that described a novel approach to reconstructing oral defects like Jack's.[19,20] The authors described using cartilage from the dog's ear flap to implant in the defect, providing a framework for the mucosa to grow over the cartilage and allow for complete healing. She showed us the paper; the authors had only used the technique in one case, but we were fascinated by the idea. Although neither of us had done anything like this before, it might be what Jack needed. By using tissue from his own body, the chances of rejection of the graft were minimal, and we could design the implant to fit into the defect. We presented the unusual surgical plan to the owners to see what they thought.

The owners were game to try the cartilage graft technique. Two weeks after his initial operation, Jack was again admitted to the hospital for his second surgery (third if you include the biopsy of the mass). Despite the problems with his mouth, he was in good spirits, had been eating well, and surprisingly did not have any foul odors from his mouth.

Jack was anesthetized and positioned for surgery on his mouth like his previous procedure. But this time, the first incision was made on the inside of his earflap to harvest the cartilage graft. In dogs and cats, two thin sheets of cartilage form the shape of the flap. The cartilage adds stiffness to the flap and allows the ear muscles to move the ear around to hear better. The sheets are the same size and shape, like two slices of sandwich bread. Becky delicately cut and removed a rectangular piece of one of the cartilage sheets. The part that she removed was designed to fit the defect in Jack's mouth. The graft was sutured in place in Jack's mouth. Another hole remained near the one that we grafted, but we decided against trying to close it since the tissues seemed to be under tension. A basic rule of surgery is not to attempt closure of tissues under tension since they will likely pull apart and not heal properly. We would allow the area grafted with cartilage to heal first and repair the remaining defect later.

In addition to the revision and grafting of his mouth incision, we placed an esophagostomy tube in Jack. This tube entered his neck and traveled down the esophagus almost to his stomach. The tube allowed Jack's owners to feed him and give oral medications without the food and pills going into his mouth, where it could disrupt the graft. Feeding tubes are a standard device in dogs and cats that are either not eating or have had surgery on the mouth. The esophagostomy tube in Jack had the same function as the PEG tube in Charlie but was placed in a different location. The tube can be left in for several days or even weeks if necessary. When no longer needed, it's pulled out, and then the dog or cat can eat and drink normally as before.

Jack did well after his revision surgery and went home the next day. Several days after the cartilage graft surgery, he returned to the hospital for a recheck exam. He was doing well, eating fine, and feeling good. He was having problems drinking water, likely because the water was getting up into his nose since there was still a remaining hole that we hadn't fixed yet. His ear was healing; there was a small amount of swelling, probably due to a seroma —accumulation of fluid under the skin incision that would likely resolve on its own in a few more days. We examined his mouth, and although the grafted area was healing well, there was a small hole in the middle of the cartilage implant, about one millimeter in diameter. We weren't sure why that had developed but hoped the tissue could still fill in the opening since it healed so well everywhere else around the graft.

Since Jack was having some difficulty drinking water, we still felt that the remaining defect in his mouth would need to be closed, but we wanted to wait a little longer for the cartilage graft to heal completely. He wasn't having any other significant problems, so we were comfortable giving it a little more time.

Third Time Was the Charm

A few weeks later, Jack presented to us again for another surgery, the third major operation to reconstruct his mouth. We planned to make another flap out of his tissue adjacent to the opening and swing it like a door to cover it. It would be a tricky procedure but much less so than the original surgery to remove the tumor. We considered another cartilage graft, but the hole was too big. We hoped this would be his final surgery, and of course, so did his owners. But there was some risk. If this flap did not successfully close the opening, there were no other good options for reconstructing it. The tissues around the incision were tight with scar tissue and not ideal for making into a flap. We had to construct this mucosal flap very carefully to maintain a good blood supply and be sutured over the defect without any tension under the sutures.

Jack was placed under general anesthesia, and we prepared his mouth for the surgery. As in the first surgery, Becky used a sterile surgical marking pen to outline the proposed incisions to make the flap. The tissues were incised, and the flap was constructed. It remained attached to one side of the gum and then flipped like a swinging door to cover the opening. Sutures were placed, and the flap did not seem to be under much tension. Jack recovered well from anesthesia.

The day after his surgery, Jack looked good and was discharged from the hospital. It was amazing how quickly he recovered from all the surgeries. He seemed undaunted by the whole process; his attitude was good, and his tail never stopped wagging. He was a remarkable dog, such a trooper through all this. But his ordeal was not quite over—some unexpected complications arose after this procedure.

Four days after the flap surgery, Jack's owners were concerned. He was not acting like himself, seemed lethargic, and was not eating as much as usual. They brought him to the hospital in the evening and saw one of the emergency doctors. Jack was anesthetized to allow a complete examination of this mouth and throat. The flap was intact, but it was infected, with a small amount of pus coming from the incision. Infection in the mouth after surgery is very rare. The tissues have a rich blood supply, and the inside of the mouth is constantly being cleaned by saliva.

Since the flap was still holding, more surgery would thankfully not be necessary. However, infection tends to delay healing.[11] We were concerned that anything slowing down the healing of the flap incisions could still lead to a breakdown and then another operation. Time would tell. Jack was prescribed antibiotics for the infection, and the owners were instructed to rinse his mouth with an oral disinfectant.

Jack did well at home for several more days and seemed to be on the road to recovery. But about one week after developing the infection, he started having a different problem. He again became more sluggish and, at random times, would jump and yelp in pain. The episodes didn't appear to be triggered by eating or touching his mouth, but he was clearly in some distress when they occurred. The owners were very concerned—it's not easy to see your pet be in obvious pain.

His owners brought Jack to the clinic for Becky to examine. She was able to look into his mouth without anesthesia and was relieved to see that the flap looked good. It did not appear infected and was healing well, although some small areas of ulceration of the gum were seen where the flap had been created. His lower molar teeth did not appear to be interfering with the sensitive tissues around the incision, a problem that commonly occurs after this kind of surgery. During the exam, Jack opened his mouth widely, and he suddenly cried in pain. Something was causing irritation and discomfort.

Although there was no way to prove it, our theory was that some nerve endings in the area where the flap originated were exposed and caused Jack's sensitivity. The ulcer in the gums could be contributing to the pain as well. There was nothing we could do surgically to cover the nerves or fix the ulcers. Becky prescribed Gabapentin, an analgesic drug that is particularly good for neurogenic pain. We hoped that would give Jack some relief while the area healed and the nerves were no longer exposed.

Two weeks later, Jack came in for a recheck oral exam. He was doing better but still had occasional pain in his mouth. The incisions continued to heal, and the flap had not broken down. All this was good news; now, we just hoped Jack would finally get back to normal.

Almost three months went by before we saw Jack again. There had been no bad news from the owners during this time, so we hoped that all was going well. We sedated Jack and looked at his mouth. It looked great! All the incisions were now completely healed. No remaining holes were going into his nasal cavity, and we found no evidence of tumor regrowth. Jack could finally be treated like a normal dog again. His owners were pleased, and so were we.

A Cancer Survivor

It was a four-month ordeal for this lovable, affectionate golden retriever. From biopsies and major surgery to additional surgeries to fix unhealed areas to enduring frequent pain in his mouth, it had been a trying time for Jack, his owners, and us. But through it all, he never lost his wonderful personality. Tail wagging, tongue licking, and begging for attention, he was a fantastic dog. Through it all, he never seemed defeated, never looked back. He just kept being true to himself, a people-loving, happy-go-lucky golden retriever.

I spoke with Noel, Jack's mom, at the time of this writing. Jack lived another six years after his surgeries. She said he had no residual effects of the operations on his mouth, and the tumor never returned. He remained healthy until the age of ten when old age set in, and he developed some debilitating issues that necessitated euthanasia. She said he was the most wonderful dog they'd ever had, and they missed him terribly. "Not a day goes by that we don't think about him," she said. After he was gone, one of the saddest things was not to see him do his usual early morning routine of delivering stuffed animals or their shoes to them.

Noel said that Jack's oral surgery ordeal enhanced their bond with him. She vividly remembered doing the required nursing care during that challenging four-month period. It made her appreciate him even more and live each day grateful that he was a part of their lives.

When I reflect on Jack, his multiple surgeries, and his recovery, I marvel at one crucial aspect of his story: the remarkable knowledge and skill of his primary surgeon, my wife, Dr. Ball. In this case, I was strictly the assistant—Becky performed the surgeries and directed his postoperative care. As I watched her work on Jack's mouth with each surgery, her surgical abilities were evident. She carefully planned the procedures, including reviewing the anatomy and surgical technique and making necessary measurements to construct the mucosal flaps. She had never done a bilateral maxillectomy before, and neither of us had done an ear cartilage graft before. She adhered to essential basic surgical principles like gentle tissue handling and controlling bleeding. After each surgery, the patient care she provided for Jack was impeccable, on a par with what would be done for a person in the hospital.

A good doctor can learn from other innovators and think creatively about solving medical problems. They can make effective and timely decisions for their patients based on a combination of fundamental principles taught in school, available medical literature describing the results of clinical research, and, most importantly, common sense. All these elements came into play for Jack, and his primary surgeon used them all. That is why Jack was a cancer survivor and spent many more years with his loving owners.

Chapter 7: Bob

When I married my wife Becky, I also married Bob. It was a package deal. From the beginning of my relationship with Becky, I recognized how important Bob was to her. If Bob and I had not gotten along, guess who would have been kicked to the curb? (Hint: not Bob!) He was an integral part of her life, and over the next several years he would become a big part of mine as well.

When Becky adopted Bob, he was a two-year-old mixed breed, mostly Labrador retriever. A large, stocky dog, robust rather than lanky or skinny, he was the kind of dog you could playfully thump on his side without hurting him. He had a beautiful light brown coat that was soft and thick. Becky had rescued him from an animal shelter in Georgia while serving in the Army Veterinary Corps. Two other families had adopted him and then returned him to the animal shelter for various reasons. Immediately after meeting him, Becky fell in love. The fact that others had rejected him only made her want him more. As time went on, that love would grow stronger.

Bob was affectionate and thrived on attention, but he didn't demand it. He didn't jump on you, smother your face, or act hyperactive and annoying. Bob was polite about his requests for affection; he was a gentleman. While you were sitting in a chair, he would slowly walk up and nuzzle your hand until it rested on his head where he wanted to be scratched. He had a petting strategy, and it worked.

Bob was a sensitive creature, which seemed at odds with his large size and commanding bark. He was easily frightened and had a low pain threshold. With even the slightest bump, he sometimes would scream. This vulnerability was yet another characteristic that endeared Bob to Becky.

Bob would put on quite a show when strangers came to the house. His bark was loud, and some people were frightened by it. He would stand up on his hind legs when he barked to make the display even more intimidating. We called this his "kangaroo bark." The funny thing was that once people he didn't know came inside and sat down, he would abruptly stop barking and leave them alone. I guess he figured they were staying despite his tough guy act, so he might as well give it up. I never saw him bite anyone, so the cliché "his bark is worse than his bite" was accurate for Bob.

When Becky and I first started dating, Bob did the kangaroo bark at me when I came over to her house. This went on for the first few weeks of me entering his world. I stayed in the category of an unknown stranger for quite some time. Then one day, the barking abruptly stopped; Bob had accepted me, and we started to be friends. As Bob's story unfolds over the next several years, we would become much closer.

The first time I visited Becky and Bob in her house, I noticed shreds of magazine paper all over the living room floor. I was a little worried that Bob had done something terrible by grabbing a magazine off the coffee table and chewing it up while Becky was away. Then I noticed a basket on the floor with a large stack of old magazines in it. Becky explained that Bob preferred magazines instead of chewing on bones or toys. I had never seen that before. After a while, I realized it was a nightly ritual for him. While we watched TV, he would slowly walk to the magazine basket and carefully choose one out of the pile. It wasn't always the one on top; he preferred certain magazines. One of them was the Victoria's Secret magazine. (I was always sad to see that one destroyed.) Then he would spend hours slowly chewing the paper into little bits and shreds. He didn't eat the pages, just chewed them and spit them out on the floor. As unusual as it was, it seemed to comfort and calm him. After he was done, sometimes a few pieces of paper would be stuck to his lips, making for a very strange-looking dogface indeed.

He Was More Than a Pet

The relationship between Bob and Becky was beyond close. They did the usual things that a dog and his owner do: play together, snuggle on the couch, and take walks together. But their connection was deeper. They sensed each other's feelings and moods. Becky is gifted in reading dogs' signals, body language, facial expressions, and sounds. She was particularly good at picking up on Bob's needs and desires. I think he sensed her moods and feelings as well. Their connection was almost spiritual. Although some may call this telepathy, a more reasonable conclusion might be that dogs have incredible senses and can use them to understand or read their owners.[17] We've already talked about their sense of smell, but dogs are also very aware of our tone of voice, facial expression, and body language. That kind of intimate communication was obvious between Bob and Becky.

One of the many things reflecting the closeness of their relationship was the vast array of nicknames that Becky gave to Bob. Here is a sampling of the list: Mr. Bees, Robert Bob Todd, Licky McLickerton, B-Bob-a-loo Bob, and most comical of all: Toothpaste Tony and His Twin Engine Turboplane. I thought nicknames were supposed to be shorter versions of one's name!

Becky and Bob also had a lot in common. Bob was an introvert, just like Becky. They both preferred a quiet night at home watching TV rather than going out on the town. They both were uncomfortable with strangers, although they acted this out differently. I never saw Becky do the kangaroo bark. Their circle of friends was small, but they both craved intimacy with their loved ones. More than anything, they needed to be with people they could trust and love. Becky and Bob gave new meaning to the "human-animal bond."

At first, I wasn't sure how to fit into this little family. I knew one thing for sure—I wasn't going to force my way in. Patience and sensitivity were required. As Becky and I became closer, I needed to respect Bob's place and ensure that he didn't feel threatened by my presence. It was a delicate and slow process, but gradually Bob accepted me as part of the family. I'll never forget the first time Bob wagged his tail when I came to visit Becky instead of giving me the kangaroo bark. I had arrived!

The First Hint of Trouble

It wasn't long after Becky, Bob, and I started living together that we noticed a lump on his left front leg. It was just under the skin, about the size of a large grape, halfway between his elbow and wrist. One of the first things surgeons do when they see a lump in an animal is to put their hand on it, move it around and pick it up, and get their fingers beneath it. They do this to see if the mass could be removable and if there would be enough skin to close the incision after its removal. This lump seemed to be kind of stuck to the surrounding tissues: it was not very movable on palpation. Soon after discovering the lump, Becky did a type of biopsy called a fine needle aspirate, a simple procedure involving sticking a small hypodermic needle into the mass to get some cells. The material is smeared on a glass slide and then submitted to a pathologist for a diagnosis. The report came back with no evidence of cancer, just some fat cells and debris. This was a relief. Now we could just keep an eye on it. No need to do anything unless it changed.

It did change. It got bigger. In a few weeks, it had almost doubled in size. We became concerned because a benign tumor shouldn't grow that fast. There was no choice but to remove it surgically and send the tissue to a pathologist to see if it was cancer. Becky was working as a surgeon in a specialty clinic in Indianapolis, so that's where the surgery would happen.

After performing routine diagnostic tests to ensure Bob was a good candidate for anesthesia, the surgery was scheduled. Becky and her technician put him under anesthesia, and his leg was clipped and prepared for sterile surgery. Bob was moved into the surgery room, and the leg was draped in for the surgical excision. Becky made an elliptical incision in the skin around the tumor, standard for this procedure. She began to dissect the tumor and separate it from the surrounding tissues of his leg, such as the muscle, blood vessels, and nerves in the immediate vicinity. That's when the trouble began. The tumor was not confined to a small nodule of tissue. It was attached and growing into the adjacent fascia, muscles, and bones of his leg. It was an invasive tumor. This was a disheartening discovery because this kind of tumor behavior indicates a malignant rather than benign tumor. It is much more difficult, and frequently impossible, to get the whole tumor out when it's attached to everything around it. Leaving even a few microscopic tumor cells behind will result in re-growth and possibly spreading of the tumor both in the same place and into other areas of the body.

Becky was devastated when she discovered that the tumor was invasive. She continued with the surgery, but it had become clear that this lump was most likely cancer, and she was getting more and more upset as time went on. She removed as much of the tumor as possible and then stitched up his leg. Tears rolled down her face as she finished closing his skin.

Becky placed a bandage on Bob's leg and then transferred him to his cage in the clinic. He recovered well from the anesthesia and surgery, and once he was fully awake, we took him home. We gave him his pain medication and then bedded him down for the night, or so we thought. He did not have a restful night. He moaned and groaned all night long, getting little rest. He couldn't get settled; he would lie down for a while, then abruptly get up and pace around the bedroom and the house. It was a fitful night for everyone, and the whole family felt the effects of sleep deprivation the next day. Even our cat Wally was seriously annoyed by the whole situation.

The next day Bob slowly got back to normal and thankfully was fine by nightfall and even got a good night's sleep. Everybody's routine eventually got back on track. Now we just had to wait for the pathology results on the tumor. The report came back five days after the surgery. It was not good news; the tumor was a high-grade soft tissue sarcoma, a very malignant cancer, and the surgical margins were dirty, meaning there were still cancer cells in his leg. This was a serious situation for Bob and a lot of stress and anxiety for his mom and me. Now what?

I knew that Becky would insist on doing everything possible for her beloved Mr. Bees. We consulted with one of the veterinary oncologists at Ohio State to find out the next step to fight this cancer. He recommended radiation therapy, like what Billy Bob had on her nose in Chapter 5. It would be eighteen daily treatments of his leg performed at Ohio State on Monday through Friday, taking weekends off. The treatments would therefore last almost a month. He would need to be anesthetized for each treatment to keep him still. There would likely be complications of the therapy, such as inflammation and swelling of the irradiated skin and leg. We would need to place a clean dressing on the area after each therapy session. Bob would probably also need pain relievers during the therapy.

Friends on a Journey Together

Since Becky was working in Indianapolis and I was at Ohio State in Columbus, I took care of Bob during the radiation treatments. I was a little nervous about this. Remember what I said about the intensity of the relationship between Bob and Becky. If anything happened to him under my watch, well, I think you know what I'm getting at. The plan was to have him in Columbus for his treatments from Monday through Friday, then drive him to Indy, a two-and-a-half-hour drive, to spend the weekends with his mom. Becky would miss him terribly during the week and instructed me to send frequent updates on his daily activities.

Bob tolerated the radiation therapy ordeal surprisingly well. Each day he was anesthetized, irradiated, and woken up quickly. During the treatments, I went about my usual faculty activities in clinics: attending rounds with my students, seeing patients in the Veterinary Teaching Hospital, doing surgeries, etc. After the therapy sessions, I returned Bob to his run. He could move around in this large, enclosed area, and it was near my ward where all my in-patients were housed. It was clear to everyone that Bob knew me; during rounds, every time I walked past his run, he would jump up, wag his tail, and trot up to the front of the run to see me. Everyone else who walked by him got the infamous kangaroo bark.

Bob and I developed a routine during these treatments. After the therapy session, I applied a clean dressing on his leg. Bandaging the affected leg was essential to protect the radiation area from trauma, sun exposure, and tongue (licking the site is not allowed). Then it was feeding time and out to the small animal exercise area for some sunshine and taking care of bodily business. Bob and I were developing a relationship. We were on this journey together, and our bond deepened every day. Each evening I took him to Becky's rental home in Columbus that she still had under lease even though she had moved to Indianapolis. Bob felt very comfortable at that house, and I think spending the nights there helped him get needed rest and recovery between treatments. Most people undergoing radiation for cancer will tell you that it is physically and emotionally draining.

Fridays became Bob's favorite day of the week because we would drive west to Indianapolis and spend the weekend with Becky. It was fun to watch their weekly reunions. I couldn't tell which one of them was more excited. The love they shared was beautiful.

Mondays, we would get up very early and make the trip back to Columbus to start the radiation routine over again. With each treatment, the irradiated area on his leg became more inflamed and irritated. The skin looked sunburned and began to ooze a yellowish fluid. These were expected complications of the treatments, but I felt terrible for Bob, knowing it must have been uncomfortable. I started using petroleum impregnated gauze bandages on the affected skin, hoping they would soothe the angry-looking area. These bandages worked well because they didn't adhere to the inflamed area, making the dressing changes less uncomfortable.

Finally, the radiation treatments were over, and Bob could return permanently to Becky in her little house in Indianapolis. He was happy to be there and not make the trek east to Columbus the following Monday. The leg bandages would continue for several more days until the irradiated area healed. If the leg was left exposed too soon, Bob would probably lick the area excessively, which could result in a lick granuloma, a chronically inflamed firm lesion on the leg that would take additional treatment and persist for a long time.

Bob's leg healed completely, and we continued to monitor the area for any signs of re-growth of the tumor. The radiation therapy left a rectangular hairless and pinkish scar on the leg. After many months with no problems, we honestly began to forget about it. The doctor in us knew you could seldom use the words cancer and cure in the same sentence, but the pet owner and Bob lover in us were hoping against hope that we had knocked this tumor out and it would no longer be a problem. Eventually, we would find out that the fight was not over yet, not by a long shot.

The Cancer Survivor as Ring-Bearer

One year after the surgery to remove the tumor on his leg, the cancer came back. The new tumor developed a couple of centimeters outside the area that had been treated with radiation. The radiation had not killed all tumor cells, and now they had grown into a subcutaneous tumor, about the size of a small grape. No playing wait and see with this situation—we planned to remove the tumor as soon as possible. We were now living in Minneapolis, working for one of the Blue Pearl veterinary specialty hospitals in Eden Prairie. We took Bob into the clinic, ran routine blood tests and radiographs, anesthetized him, and removed the new tumor. He recovered well and went home that night. Luckily, he had a much more restful night than after the first tumor surgery.

The recurrent tumor was, as expected, a fibrosarcoma, but this time the pathologists called it a low-grade tumor. We weren't sure what to make of this report since the original tumor had been high grade. Had it changed somehow to a lower malignancy behavior? We certainly hoped so, but the fact that it recurred outside of the field of radiation therapy was concerning. Bob's cancer was very much back on our radar.

Even as Bob's tumor was on our minds, we did have other distractions occupying our attention. Becky and I began to prepare for our wedding in July of 2011. We were married in Hocking Hills, Ohio, in an outdoor ceremony with a small group of family and friends. Bob was an essential participant in the event and was included in the pictures taken that day. He was the ceremonial ring bearer and as such played a very important part in the nuptials. Many people asked about the hairless area on his leg. It was a reminder to all of us that Bob was still battling cancer but doing well otherwise and enjoying the events of the day. He got lots of attention and TLC from everyone; he did no kangaroo barking that day.

After the wedding, we headed back to Minneapolis and got back into our daily routine. All was well with Bob, with no problems with his leg and no tumors. We played ball in the backyard and went on long walks. We hunkered down for another long cold season on the Minnesota tundra as winter approached. Then, in December, eight months after the first tumor recurrence on Bob's leg, we found another one. This one was also outside of the area that had been irradiated.

It was becoming clear there were still abundant cancer cells in his leg. Soon after finding this second tumor recurrence, we surgically removed it the same way as we had the other two. Histopathology of this one was also a fibrosarcoma. In a year and a half, we had now operated on Bob three times for this cancer in his leg. Each time the tumor re-grew, it was farther up his leg, probably following the lymphatic vessels as they drained the lower parts of the limb where the tumor had started. It was just a matter of time before it would come back again, and at some point, it could spread to other organs. We began to consider the option of leg amputation.

A Difficult Decision

Becky and I have recommended amputation on some of our patients, both dogs and cats, for various disorders. Severe trauma, necrosis from bite wounds, severe infection that threatens to cause septicemia, and cancer are some of the issues that may require amputation. Although it sounds drastic to many owners, we try to assure them that dogs and cats usually do very well on three legs. They can continue doing most of the things that dogs and cats love to do—walk, run, play, chase a ball, go up and down stairs, and use a litterbox—all without assistance. If it's a rear leg amputated in a male dog, the only thing they can't do is hike up the other back leg when they urinate.

Although a leg prosthesis is standard in humans after amputation, they are not very practical for dogs and cats. Animals don't tolerate foreign objects attached to their bodies; they try to shake them off or will lick and chew on them. Besides, dogs and cats do so well on three legs we usually don't recommend a prosthesis unless it's the unusual situation where the animal has already lost one leg and may need another one removed.

We seriously considered amputation to treat Bob's cancer, but this was Bob. He was not like other dogs; he was sensitive, freaked out easily over little things, and didn't always recover smoothly from anesthesia. There could be blood loss, incisional complications, and infection. Although dogs do very well with just one rear leg, they carry more weight on the front legs, and big dogs could have difficulty getting around on one front leg, especially older and arthritic ones. All these considerations swirled around in our heads as we wrestled with the decision.

After thinking it over carefully, we decided the only way to control his cancer was to remove the leg. We knew that Bob would need lots of pain control after surgery and assistance during rehabilitation. Even with potent analgesic drugs, there would be moaning, whimpering, and maybe even some screaming (from Bob and us!). Just getting him to stand after surgery would be onerous. But he was otherwise healthy, in good body condition, and a good candidate for anesthesia and surgery. I was honestly a little more worried about how Becky would handle the surgery than how Bob would.

Becky asked me to do the amputation. She was too emotionally involved with this patient. It's much harder to keep a clear head when it's your own pet. I had done many of them over the years and was comfortable with the procedure. But, again, this was Bob, the dog that meant the world to the woman I loved. I don't often get apprehensive about doing surgery, but this one, I must be honest, made me nervous. I wanted everything to go smoothly. Becky entrusted me to do a major operation on her beloved friend.

The practice we were working in had two offices, one in Eden Prairie and the other in Blaine, Minnesota. The clinic in Blaine had a nice, large operating room that we liked, and we would do the surgery there. Preoperative blood tests and a CT scan of Bob's chest were performed the day before surgery and were normal, showing no evidence of tumors anywhere else in his body. The cancer seemed to be confined to his leg. It was time to take a big step forward in ridding Bob of this persistent and aggravating tumor.

On the morning of surgery, Bob got to drink a little water but, of course, no food. He was not happy about that as mealtime was very important to this big dog with a big appetite. We drove him to the clinic and got him settled into his large cage. Everyone there knew him, and they all fussed over him and wished him well. After getting the anesthesia equipment set up, we were ready to start. Drug dosages were calculated and drawn up, and the surgery room was fully equipped and organized. Becky supervised the induction and maintenance of anesthesia. At the same time, I started clipping and prepping his entire left leg for the surgery. The surgery we planned to do is called a forequarter amputation, where all the bones and muscles of the leg, including the uppermost bone called the scapula, were removed. This gave us the best chance for complete removal of his cancer.

We moved him into the surgery room on a gurney. Becky decided not to go in with him. She would stand vigil outside the treatment room and wait until the procedure was done. Even with well-performed amputations, there will be some bleeding, especially in big dogs. Many large muscles must be cut, and the blood vessels will bleed until they are either tied off or cauterized. Even though she was a surgeon, it would be stressful for her to see the blood knowing it was her Bob. If any blood managed to get on the surgery room floor or other areas, I instructed the technicians to immediately clean it up. If Becky looked in the door window, I wanted her to know that all was well.

In addition to incising through muscles, many nerves had to be transected. The group of peripheral nerves that control the front leg in dogs and cats is called the brachial plexus. It comprises six large nerves. Each of the nerves was injected with a local anesthetic, or nerve block, before being severed. The agent injected is the same that dentists use to prevent the pain of dental procedures. The nerve blocks, in addition to the other painkillers we would give Bob postoperatively, would hopefully keep him comfortable after surgery. We wanted to do everything we could to keep him from moaning and whimpering all night as he usually did after anesthesia and surgery.

The amputation went well, and Bob had an uneventful recovery from anesthesia. We placed a padded bandage over his chest to protect the incision and then moved him to his large cage, where he would spend the night. We placed his favorite stuffed animal next to him to provide comfort and companionship. Becky wrote up his treatment orders which included giving him a constant intravenous infusion of fentanyl. He would receive this all night long as well as other pain relievers. Taking him home right after such a major surgery would not have been advisable for Bob or us. He would be in a very comfortable bed in his cage and monitored closely by the technicians on duty. Since he likely would not get up to urinate overnight, we placed an indwelling urinary catheter in him to collect his urine. It was hard to leave Bob and head home, but we knew he was in good hands with the doctors and technicians who would be there all night to care for him.

The next day Bob was groggy but seemed comfortable. He didn't want to get up and needed a lot of encouragement and help to stand and move around. We used a padded sling with handles and placed it under his chest to support him while he tried to walk. But he was alert, his vital signs were good, and his incision looked fine, so we decided to take him home where he would be more comfortable in familiar surroundings. Clearly, his recovery was going to be a prolonged process. Many dogs are able walk very soon after amputation, sometimes even the next day. Not Bob: he was unsure of himself, probably still in pain, under the influence of potent analgesics, and generally needed a lot of attention and emotional support.

Getting him into the car was no easy task either. We had prepared the back end of the Subaru Outback for him with a well-padded, clean dog bed. We carefully picked him up, placed him in the car, and headed home. Becky had made our guestroom into Bob's at-home hospital room. She put the guest room bed mattress on the floor to make it easier for him to get on and off it. It had clean blankets, and his water and food dishes were close. Urinary catheters and syringes were readily available. With him not yet able to walk or go outside to relieve himself, we would have to catheterize his urinary bladder several times a day and remove the urine with a syringe. If he were a human, he'd have had a bedpan, but that's not a viable option for a dog.

He Became a Dog Again

Bob slowly improved every day and started getting his strength and confidence back. There was gradually less moaning and whimpering when I got him up and used the sling to help him walk. Finally, about three days after coming home, together, we made it outside, and he was able to relieve himself in the backyard. I immediately took his picture and texted Becky with the news. Bob was becoming a dog again. It was a day of great celebration.

After that momentous day, Bob improved more rapidly and was even willing to get up and walk independently without the sling. One evening he crawled over to the magazine basket on his own and picked out a magazine for his evening chewing ritual. Returning to his nightly entertainment routine made us sigh in relief; all was right with Bob. When the usual Minnesota winter weather began covering the backyard with a thick blanket of snow, we worried he would have trouble navigating the terrain. Surprisingly, he had no problem and even started running around and playing despite the snow and ice.

I have a short video of Bob, on three legs, retrieving his ball with Becky through several inches of snow. I have used it many times to convince owners that amputating a dog's leg rarely slows them down.

Bob's progress was a welcome sign, not only for his sake but because he was about to have a new playmate. Six weeks after his amputation, our son Stuart was born. We assured Bob that he would still be getting lots of attention even with the new miniature human crawling around. We closely monitored their activities together, and Bob quickly accepted the latest member of the family without feelings of jealousy. Bob adapting to being three-legged (we called him the Tripod) and welcoming Stuart into the family made the bond between Bob and Becky that much stronger. His entire life, Becky surrounded Bob with love and affection. She made him know he was an essential part of our family. He would never re-live the rejection he had suffered many years ago.

In less than two years, Bob had five surgeries, four of which were for leg cancer, and eighteen radiation treatments. He had to cope with three moves, a new dad, and a new baby. He somehow adapted, made the best of his situation, and moved on. Not bad for a dog who was extremely sensitive and easily scared. Eleven months after his amputation, we moved to Indianapolis, and Bob quickly settled in. He liked his new digs. He had his own room in the front of the house with big windows for him to survey his territory. He would let every dog walking down the street know this was now Bob's house.

A Reminder That He Still Had Cancer

From January 2012 to January 2015, we celebrated three anniversaries of Bob's amputation and being cancer-free. During that time, he had no surgeries or other medical treatments other than routine health maintenance. He deserved this disease-free period where he could concentrate on enjoying life and being a dog. He did a lot of backyard romping, took occasional walks around the neighborhood, and yes, enjoyed a nightly selection of a tasty magazine. We didn't want to hold our hopes too high, but the prolonged period with no evidence of cancer made us wonder if it was finally gone for good. Unfortunately, it wasn't.

In June of 2015, a lime-sized mass appeared under the skin just in front of where his leg had been amputated. It was easily palpable, movable, and not painful. Becky did a needle biopsy of it and, yet again, it was the fibrosarcoma. His old nemesis had now spread to the prescapular lymph node, one of the nodes that drain lymph from the front leg. I thought I had removed that lymph node when I did the amputation, but I hadn't. Soon after the biopsy report came in, I surgically removed the node. I sent it off for analysis by the pathologist. They confirmed that it was fibrosarcoma in the lymph node. It had taken Bob's cancer three and a half years to show up again. But we weren't ready to give up, and neither was Bob.

We consulted with the veterinary oncologist that we worked with in the clinic. She recommended treating Bob with chemotherapy using a drug called carboplatin, a potent drug commonly used for cancer in dogs. It can have side effects such as nausea, diarrhea, and bone marrow toxicity, causing low white blood cells and platelets in the blood. But since Bob's cancer had now spread to his lymph nodes, we felt that it would be worthwhile to do chemo. He had already been through a lot, but he was feeling fine, and he had been in remission for a long time. We didn't want to give up, and we were pretty sure he didn't either.

The carboplatin was given intravenously every three weeks for a total of four treatments. In between treatments, Bob was given medication for nausea and pain, and blood samples were regularly obtained to monitor his white blood cell and platelet counts. The first few treatments went well, with Bob showing no signs of severe side effects. Dogs generally tolerate chemotherapy better than people—they don't lose all their hair and have fewer complications overall. Bob was an excellent example of that. He maintained a good appetite, was active and energetic, and continued his signature activities such as magazine chewing and kangaroo barking.

After the first two treatments, Bob's white blood cell count dropped significantly. The white blood cells, particularly the neutrophils, are essential to combat infection in the body. When they drop too low, animals are prone to infections, such as pneumonia, which can become severe. We lowered the chemotherapy dosage, and Bob was given antibiotics. He weathered yet another storm and was able to finish out the final carboplatin treatment protocol. Now we just had to wait and see if it had been effective.

How Much Can He Endure?

We didn't have to wait long before another problem arose, this one unrelated to Bob's cancer but just as serious. One week after his last dose of chemotherapy, Bob seemed fine all day but was restless and panting heavily by the evening. Becky was putting our son Stuart to bed while I watched TV in the family room. Bob kept pacing back and forth between rooms and finally plopped down on the floor looking very distressed and uncomfortable. I went to him and immediately noticed that his belly was severely bloated and getting bigger by the minute. I tapped on his abdomen, and it sounded like a drum. Bob was trapping air in his stomach, the first stage of gastric dilatation-volvulus (GDV), the same condition that had affected Rip in Chapter 1. I yelled up to Becky to come down, then quickly put my coat on, loaded Bob in the car, and drove him to the clinic where we worked. Becky called ahead to let them know we were on our way and to get things ready for emergency surgery. At least for the time being, she would stay home to take care of Stuart while I got things started with Bob's treatment.

As soon as we arrived, the technicians placed an intravenous catheter in Bob to administer fluids. We then quickly obtained radiographs of his abdomen, which confirmed GDV. It was the most enormous air-filled stomach I'd seen, and it was flipped over in the typical fashion of a GDV stomach. To remove the air from his stomach, I placed a large needle directly into the stomach through the skin. The air rushed out, sounding like an air-filled balloon with a hole in it. Bob immediately looked better after removing the air from his stomach; he was more comfortable and had better mucous membrane color. We needed to get him under anesthesia and start the surgery to move the stomach back to its normal position. The longer we waited, the greater the chance his stomach would be permanently damaged like Rip's had been.

I texted Bob's radiographic images to Becky and then told her we were getting him under anesthesia. She desperately wanted to be with him. She called a friend to come to watch Stuart so she could head into the clinic. Things moved quickly, and by the time she made it to the clinic, I had Bob in surgery with the abdomen open. I put the stomach back into its normal position and performed a gastropexy, as we had done for Rip, to prevent future recurrences of GDV.

All things considered, the surgery on Bob went very well. Since we had gotten him into surgery very quickly after the GDV developed, his stomach was not damaged by the episode. I also found no other significant problems with the other organs in Bob's abdomen, which was a relief considering his fight with cancer. After closing his incision, we got him set up in the ICU, wrote treatment orders, and then stayed with him until he was awake. He recovered from anesthesia smoothly, and within a short time he was stable enough that we could leave him in the hands of the nighttime staff. A scary and exhausting evening had ended.

The following day Bob looked excellent. He was up and around, drinking and even eating a little bit, and immediately started wagging his tail when he saw me. I took some videos of him to send to Becky and let her know that her Bobby was bouncing back quickly from his ordeal the night before. Later that evening, I brought him home with me; needless to say, he and his mom were both so glad he was home.

Gastric dilatation-volvulus is a complicated disorder of the stomach in dogs that develops due to a myriad of factors and predispositions. One of the most important things we know about the condition is that any stress to a dog can make them pant, and as a result, swallow air. Aerophagia is air in the stomach. In large dogs, like Bob, prone to GDV, aerophagia initiates the dilation and then rotation of the stomach. Age is also a factor, with the syndrome being more common in older dogs. Bob had several elements that contributed to his GDV. He was a large dog, older (fourteen years old), and had just undergone a four-week course of chemotherapy. Even though he handled the chemo well, it was stressful for him. Thank goodness we caught it early and got him into surgery quickly. Luckily for Bob, he lived with two veterinary surgeons.

Bob continued his rapid recovery from the GDV and in a few days was acting like his old self again. His incision healed well, and the skin staples were removed ten days after the operation. Bob had survived another bump in the road. He was a three-legged cancer survivor, and now a GDV survivor. He would live to destroy more magazines and kangaroo bark at more visitors. But unfortunately, the clock was ticking.

We'll Know When the End Is Near

Becky and I always said that we would know when Bob was seriously ill because it would be when he stopped eating. He had a ravenous appetite. That day came about five months after his GDV surgery —Bob would not eat his food. He was also becoming lethargic and seemed uncomfortable. We suspected the worst; his cancer was coming back somewhere.

We took Bob into the clinic and had the internist perform an ultrasound exam of his abdomen. The news couldn't have been worse—Bob had tumors in the liver and kidneys and fluid accumulation in the sac around the heart. The fibrosarcoma had spread and now was everywhere in his body. After a courageous fight, Bob was now dying of cancer.

Our decision on what to do was clear. The cancer was too advanced to consider treatment. More chemotherapy would not be effective, and his weakened state would probably only make him even sicker. Letting Bob live any longer with metastatic cancer would not be fair to him. He was not living a good quality of life; he had no energy, no appetite, and was in pain and deteriorating rapidly. The best course of action was to humanely euthanize him.

Saying Good-Bye

I often wondered what it would be like for Becky when we had to put Bob to sleep. I was worried about how she would cope with the loss. If it was possible for a human being and a dog to be soul mates, Becky and Bob were it. Losing him would be devastating to her. Now we were facing that reality.

She kept it together as we prepared everything for his euthanasia. We planned to do it at home, in our family room on his favorite bed on the floor right next to his basket of magazines. Becky went to a restaurant and brought back a juicy grilled steak for Bob to have as his last meal. He started to eat the steak but then stopped, indicating how sick he was. We spent some time petting and softly talking to him to make him comfortable. We then gave him a sedative through an intravenous catheter. He relaxed and went to sleep. While Becky continued to pet and talk to him with her face next to his, I slowly injected the euthanasia solution into the catheter, and Bob drifted away peacefully. We lay next to him for a very long time as the tears poured out of our eyes. Bob was gone.

After being rejected by two families as a puppy, Bob had found Becky, an owner who would give him more love than any dog has ever received. I don't think it's an exaggeration to say Bob's life went from hell to heaven when Becky brought him home. I believe Becky's love and devotion gave Bob the will to live through all the surgeries, radiation therapy, and chemotherapy. The spiritual connection between them gave Bob the comfort of knowing she would be right by his side through all the trials and tribulations. It was as though he knew that each day he survived was a day that brought her joy. The effect of love on healing was never more evident than on this special dog.

Bob had accepted me into his family and allowed me to care for him when he needed it, and I felt privileged to be his friend. The first time he greeted me with a tail wag rather than a bark, I felt a certain validation that I will never forget. Initially, I wanted Bob's acceptance for the sake of my relationship

with Becky. But as time went on, I wanted Bob's love
for the sake of my relationship with him. We built
our history together. I helped him through his fight
with cancer, and he helped me at a time in my life
when everything was changing and I needed stability.
We were good for each other.

Bob's ashes are in an urn on the mantle above
our fireplace. Etched on the urn are all the
nicknames Becky gave him over the years. She saved
his magazines, blankets, toys, and even some of his
left-over dog food, all of which are safely stored
away in a box simply labeled "Bob." His name is
mentioned whenever we talk about our history with
pets. Although there will be other dogs in our lives,
and Becky will love them, none will ever rise to the
level of Bob. He had eminent domain over Becky's
heart. It was a once-in-a-lifetime relationship.

Chapter 8: Maximus

His full name is Maximus Quintus. A healthy one-and-a-half-year-old mixed breed, he's the most affectionate of the seven cats in his household, all of whom have Latin names. He is a full-fledged member of his family. He gets along well with everyone, including all his feline roommates, one of which is his littermate. Maximus's owners adopted him when a family member found him in a box along with sixteen other kittens who had been abandoned near a racetrack. Fortunately, all the kittens found homes.

Maximus is primarily white, with hints of cream color on his face, around his ears, and down his back. He is a very handsome cat. He is a happy cat living with a family who loves him, but his life changed forever on May 12, 2017.

Maximus and the other kittens liked to run around the house like wild animals. They would chase each other, stalk inanimate objects, or just run with no particular purpose—typical daily activity in young cats. He and one of the other kittens would jump into the bathtub and play, although getting out of the slippery tub would present a challenge. On that fateful day, May 12, he jumped into the tub like he had done many times before, but this time it was full of scalding hot water.

Maximus began screaming. He desperately tried to climb out of the tub, but it was too slippery, and his wet paws could not grip the sides. His owners immediately ran to the bathroom and pulled him from the burning hot water. They dried him off with a towel and could already see the skin on his legs and paws turning bright red. He was in excruciating pain. They placed him under the faucet to run cold water on his burns, then rushed him to the emergency clinic at MedVet Toledo.

On admission, Maximus was howling in agony. All four paws were red, swollen, and bleeding. The skin on his belly and chest was bright red and already showing bruising in some areas. On initial examination, it appeared that a large area of his body was burned. The pain was so intense the emergency clinician couldn't do a complete physical examination on him. Maximus would have to be heavily sedated to perform the exam and do procedures such as placement of an intravenous catheter.

Maximus was immediately given an opioid drug, buprenorphine, for pain. The clinician then discussed the short-term plan for treatment with the owners: intravenous fluids, pain control, blood tests to assess tissue and organ damage, and bandaging of the burn wounds. Treatment would likely be intensive, prolonged, and expensive. The prognosis for survival was poor. Despite the bad news, Maximus's owner was committed to saving him and approved the treatment plan.

Many studies have been done on people with severe burns. Intensive care consisting of pain control, intravenous fluids and antibiotics, and advanced wound care with topical medications and bandages is necessary for people with burns over large parts of their body. Even with state-of-the-art care, one study found that people with greater than 40 percent of their body burned usually have a poor outcome.[21] Infection, sepsis, and multiple organ failure are common. Although few clinical studies of burned animals have been performed, it is safe to say that with at least 30 percent of his body burned, Maximus was in critical condition.[22] His future was uncertain, at best. The ER doctors warned the owner that even with providing him all the intensive care they could deliver, he might not survive.

Blood tests on Maximus showed some serious problems—he was dehydrated, and his serum potassium was high, indicating widespread cell damage. Treatment for his first day in the hospital consisted of intravenous fluids for hydration, antibiotics to prevent infection, and a continuous intravenous infusion of fentanyl for pain control.

Excruciating Pain

The next day brought more bad news. Maximus could not walk because the skin of his footpads was beginning to peel off, leaving raw tissue exposed. The burned areas on his legs, chest, and belly were becoming purple, and even the skin of his prepuce was discolored. Some of the burned skin on his chest was becoming hard and leathery. On a pain scale from one to twenty-four (one being little or no pain, twenty-four being the worst pain possible), the attending clinician listed Maximus as twenty-four.

The emergency doctors continued supportive care and gave additional drugs to reduce the excruciating pain. Lidocaine and ketamine were added to the fentanyl intravenous infusion to provide more analgesia. The dosage of fentanyl was also increased. The burn wounds were re-bandaged, and silver sulfadiazine (Silvadene) was used as a topical cream medication on the burned areas. Silver sulfadiazine is commonly used on burn patients, both animals and humans, because of its antibacterial properties. A urinary catheter was placed in Maximus to monitor his urine output and keep him from urinating on himself since he couldn't stand or move.

After sedating him, all of Maximus's burned areas were carefully clipped and cleaned. With the hair removed, the burned regions were more clearly visible—the total surface area of his burned body appeared to be close to 40 percent. His chances of recovering from this injury seemed to dwindle by the day.

More blood tests showed that Maximus's blood proteins, in particular his albumin, were already low. His blood albumin was depleted because of the severe inflammation of the damaged skin and loss of albumin-rich fluid that oozed from his wounds. Like other critically wounded animals in this book, loss of protein is common. It can result in many complications such as delayed wound healing, tissue edema, and swelling of legs and other body parts. Maximus needed to start eating to replenish the deficiency in albumin. But he was in so much pain he had no interest in food. A nasogastric tube was placed to feed a liquid diet called Clinicare. Hopefully, this would sustain him until he felt good enough to eat.

On day three, Maximus's care was transferred to my wife, Becky; she and I were the two attending surgeons at the MedVet Toledo practice. She did a complete assessment of him and his medical record and found him to be unchanged from the previous day. He was still very lethargic and unwilling to move. Even with the analgesic therapy, he was still in a great deal of pain when handled. His paws were severely swollen, the footpads were raw and intermittently bleeding, and more of his burned areas of the chest and armpits were thickened and inflamed. Becky changed Maximus's bandages under heavy sedation and applied silver sulfadiazine cream on the wounds.

Medical Grade Honey

After completing Maximus's treatments for the day, Becky called his owner, introduced herself as the new attending clinician, and updated her on Maximus's condition and progress. The owner, a neonatologist, asked if the doctors had considered using Manuka honey on his burn wounds. Manuka honey, also called Medihoney, is a brand of medical-grade honey available for purchase over the counter in pharmacies. She had used it on some of her newborn infant patients and thought it could be helpful in Maximus. Becky agreed and began applying Medihoney to all his wounds.

Manuka honey comes from bees that acquire their nectar from the Manuka bush which is native to New Zealand. It is a topical medication for wounds because of its antibiotic properties and hyperosmotic effect which reduces swelling and inflammation in the tissues.[23] Like the granulated sugar that we used to treat Hershey in Chapter 2, honey is a time-honored substance for treating severe wounds dating back thousands of years. We all hoped that it would make a difference for little Maximus—he needed all the help he could get.

Maximus's status appeared unchanged on day four of hospitalization, but he seemed to show a slight improvement in his attitude on day five. He was more alert and responsive but still would not get up and couldn't walk because of the burn wounds on his paws. Some of the burned skin on his chest and abdomen began to turn yellowish and become crusty. These areas had probably suffered a full-thickness burn injury. When the skin is burned that badly, it will likely completely die and gradually peel away, exposing the subcutaneous tissues underneath.

Since dogs' and cats' skins have different anatomy than people's, burn injury is classified differently. Most veterinarians call the injury superficial, partial, or full thickness burn instead of the first degree, second degree, or third degree scheme used in humans. In superficial burns, only the superficial layer of skin, the epidermis, is damaged. In partial-thickness burns, the epidermis and superficial layer of the dermis is affected. The entire layer of skin, including the epidermis and the entire dermis, is damaged with full-thickness burns. Maximus had areas of all three types. As the skin dies in the full-thickness burn areas, it becomes yellowish-brown and looks like leather. This leathery scab on a burn wound is called the eschar. It will gradually peel off from the body, exposing the underlying tissues.

It can take several days to determine which areas of skin have suffered either partial or full-thickness damage. Each day on Maximus, we waited to see if his wounds would "declare" themselves and indicate to us how badly injured the tissues were. Surgical removal of the dead skin should be done, but Maximus was not in good enough condition to have general anesthesia and surgery.

On day seven in the hospital, Maximus took a big step forward and began to eat. He had been getting small amounts of the liquid diet through his nasogastric tube, but now he ate some canned cat food, which was good for him and a big morale boost for his owners and doctors. Like the other animals with severe wounds we've discussed, nutrition is critical to survival in burn patients. The protein, calories, vitamins, and minerals in food are essential to healing. His blood protein levels quickly began to increase. His body was being nutritionally replenished and could start making the necessary elements for wound healing.

The "Onesie" Bandage

Maximus showed more signs of improvement in the following days. He continued to eat, he was alert and responsive, seemed to be in less pain, and his wounds were finally looking better. The severe swelling of his front legs and paws was going down, and there was less inflammation; he was beginning to get up and even take a few steps on his healing feet. The now blackish area of skin on his chest and abdomen was not larger, and it was beginning to peel away from the healthy skin around it. Maximus's increased appetite coupled with the use of Medihoney on his wounds was having positive effects. Becky also devised a clever strategy for his bandages. Because of the extent of the injuries, practically all of Maximus's body had to be bandaged. To simplify the bandage changes that were time-consuming and painful, she purchased several infant onesies to cover the entire body, legs, and feet. The onesies fit well on Maximus and covered all the wounds. Each day the onesie was removed, the wounds gently cleaned, Medihoney ointment applied, and a clean onesie put back on. The entire process was easier and faster, resulting in less stress to Maximus. The little cream and white kitty with the Latin name was putting up a good fight, but there was still a long way to go.

Maximus continued to improve, and twelve days after being admitted to MedVet Toledo, he looked good enough to be discharged. No longer needing intravenous drugs and fluids, his owners could give oral medications at home, and he was starting to walk a little. He went home with prescriptions for antibiotics, analgesics, and probiotics for his digestive tract. Before taking him home, the owners watched Becky and her assistants cleanse his wounds, apply the Medihoney, and dress him in his onesie. The required nursing care at home might have been overwhelming for any other owner. But he would be cared for by an experienced physician who was quite comfortable being his supervising doctor and home nurse. Maximus would be so much more comfortable and relaxed back in his familiar environment, something he had missed for almost two weeks.

It had been quite a twelve-day hospital ordeal for Maximus. He had been heavily sedated every day for wound care, debridement, bathing, and bandaging. He had catheters in multiple veins, including a double lumen catheter in his jugular vein, a special tube that allows blood sampling and fluid administration. He also had catheters in his urethra to collect urine and in his stomach to administer a liquid diet. For most of the twelve days, he could not walk or even get up on his feet. Four different drugs were used for pain, either alone or in combination, and three antibiotics were prescribed to combat infection. Intravenous fluids were used for most of his hospitalization to prevent dehydration. He received intravenous colloid fluids (Vetstarch) to maintain fluid balance because of low serum protein levels. Initially, silver sulfadiazine was used on his wounds, followed by medical-grade honey. His injuries were finally starting to heal, and the worst of his agony was over. But there were more chapters to be written about his fight to regain a good quality of life.

They Even Slept with Him

Maximus's care at home was challenging, even for an owner who was a physician. Since they could see how gruesome his wounds were, it was an emotionally difficult time for them. Although he was trying to walk, it was difficult, and at times the owner and her husband would have to help him get up or change the side he was lying on. Once he finally stood up, it was hard for him to lie back down, and he would sometimes fall asleep standing up. Like a human invalid, they would bring him water and food and clean him up afterward. He was not physically able to go in and out of his litter box, which of course was a serious problem. The owner made an area of absorbent paper and pads on the floor for him to urinate and defecate on, which he began to use, but at times he was so sore he couldn't even make it to that spot. Urine and feces would get on him, requiring gentle bathing to keep him and his wounds clean. Cats are clean animals but don't like to be washed—it's hard to imagine the amount of stress he was experiencing.

For several days, one of the owners slept each night by Maximus's side so they could tend to his needs throughout the night. They removed his bandages three times a day, gave him a soaking bath in the sink, and applied fresh honey and clean dressings on his wounds. Their commitment to Maximus was incredible. They gave him the same care level a burn patient would receive in a human hospital. He would not have lived without the intensive nursing they provided for him.

After six days at home, Maximus came in to see Becky for a recheck examination. He was doing surprisingly well and still had a good appetite. The dead skin on his belly and legs had gradually peeled away, exposing tissue underneath that was slowly forming granulation tissue. The owner was doing an excellent job managing the open wounds. The Medihoney was working well to prevent infection and encourage healing. In much less pain and a little more mobile, Maximus slowly made progress.

Maximus then began a schedule of recheck exams at MedVet Toledo every four or five days. His wounds slowly healed; the dead skin on his belly gradually peeled away over about three weeks, as underlying superficial skin cells tried to fill in the defect. His paws and legs also slowly improved. The burns in these areas were partial thickness, so the dead skin layers were thinner and the skin less damaged underneath. When the eschars over his Achilles tendons peeled off in the rear legs, the tendons appeared discolored and not healthy. Maximus was walking with his lower legs dropped down parallel to the ground. The Achilles is an essential tendon for rear leg function and, if damaged, severe lameness results. Becky recommended continued wound therapy with Medihoney and warned the owner that surgery to reconstruct the tendons could be necessary. Time would tell how much of the tendons were damaged and non-functional.

About a month after he went home, Maximus had another setback. His owners brought him to the Emergency Service for two swollen, fluid-filled areas, one over his right shoulder and one over his right hip. The emergency clinician sedated Maximus and lanced the fluid pocket over his shoulder, which proved to be an abscess. The swelling over his hip, also an abscess, ruptured spontaneously. These areas of infection were forming in regions that were not injured because Maximus's immune system was overwhelmed by the massive amount of burn injury. The emergency doctors treated him with antibiotics and supportive care. Thankfully he recovered quickly from this complication and was soon back home. Becky saw him a few days later; the abscessed areas were healing well, and the Achilles tendons looked better. Maximus's stance and his mobility had improved.

Maximus continued to be re-examined about every two weeks. He was making good progress; the dead areas of skin completely sloughed off, and the skin defects were healing well. Maximus was becoming a textbook case of healing by wound contraction. But there was a problem—as the skin contracted in his groin region, the scar tissue pulled his rear legs toward his body and severely restricted his mobility. When wound contraction is excessive, and the scar tissue causes problems, it is called wound contracture. Maximus was now becoming a textbook case of the *negative* effects of wound healing. It appeared that more surgery would be necessary to alleviate the contracture and allow Maximus to use his rear legs better.

In addition to this issue, Maximus had a couple of less severe complications. As his paws healed from the burns, some of his nails fell out due to tissue damage. They protruded out of the digit in an abnormal location as they grew back, causing irritation and pain. Declaw surgery would be necessary to remove the nails and relieve the pain and inflammation.

One last problem: The end of Maximus's tail had not healed from its burn injury, and the very tip of it had died and fallen off. The end of the remaining tail wasn't healing well and would become abraded and even bleed with the least amount of trauma. Some of his tail would need to be amputated.

Maximus was scheduled for general anesthesia and therapeutic declaw of two toes, tail amputation, and castration (it had not been done as a kitten). Becky performed the surgery, all procedures went well, and Maximus recovered without problems. He was discharged from the hospital the next day. Two weeks later, at recheck exam, all incisions were healed, and all sutures were removed.

Release the Legs!

Maximus Quintus was well on his way to making a full recovery from his horrible injury. His wounds were 90 percent healed, and he was eating, active, and not in pain. But there was still one remaining problem that needed attention. The wound contracture in his groin was worsening. It was like the insides of his thighs were connected to each other with tight rubber bands. He couldn't pull his rear legs out away from his body like we do when we sit cross-legged on the floor. It was a severe problem, making him hop like a rabbit when he walked. He was having trouble going in and out of the litter box. Something had to be done.

Becky had a pretty good idea of how to fix the problem, but she asked me to consult with her on Maximus to confirm her plan. We discussed some surgical options but decided to make a final decision once we saw Maximus together and could assess his situation. After seeing Maximus and making some measurements on the skin of his belly and groin area, I recommended we fix the problem with a skin flap. This would be like the type of flap we had done on Charlie in Chapter 3 but with some modifications. The construction of the flap would be the same, a sizeable tongue-shaped flap of skin would be made, but we would move the skin flap to a different location than we had on Charlie. Instead of moving the skin to the knee, we would rotate it to the middle of the groin area where the contracture had occurred. This extra skin would allow his inguinal skin to be looser and more flexible, which would give the rear legs much more mobility and comfort.

The surgery was performed on November 29, a little more than seven months after Maximus's injury. Like plastic surgery in people, we made several measurements and used a sterile marking pen to draw the incisions necessary to create the flap. We incised through the thick, inflexible scar tissue on the middle of his belly and groin area to release the contracted skin between his thighs. Immediately the rear legs began to loosen up and were much more movable. We then constructed the skin flap using a scalpel according to the diagrams drawn on Maximus. We rotated it to fill in the incision in the scar tissue. The flap gave the contracted area new, healthy skin and subcutaneous tissue to expand and keep the thighs from being bound to each other. A drain tube was placed underneath the skin to prevent fluid buildup, and all the incisions were closed with sutures. Now time would tell if the flap would survive and if Maximus could begin to use his rear legs normally.

Maximus recovered uneventfully from anesthesia, and the following day he was doing well. His skin flap was bruised but otherwise looked okay. It takes several days to know for sure if the flap will survive. There was minimal drainage from the closed suction drain. He was discharged back to his owner later that day.

Maximus came back five days after surgery to have the drain removed. There had been minimal fluid coming out of the drain, which was a good sign. There were no signs of infection, and the skin flap was swollen but looked good. Becky removed the drain, and he was sent back home. His next appointment would be to remove his stitches and make a final skin flap assessment.

Seven days later, Maximus came back for suture removal and to assess the success of his skin flap reconstruction. There is always a bit of anxiety for the surgeons when we re-evaluate animals after a surgery like this. Everything hinges on the viability of the skin flap. If this surgery was unsuccessful, Maximus could have been permanently disabled. Thankfully, the incisions were completely healed, and 100 percent of the flap was alive and well. We all breathed a sigh of relief. He was already more mobile, using his rear legs much better, and easily getting in and out of the litter box.

Maximus was now very close to being back to normal. He would have one more minor surgery to close some remaining small areas of healing skin on his back legs. Otherwise, he was doing well and rapidly regaining strength and body weight. He came in to see Becky on January 1, 2018, about seven months after his original injury, to assess all his wounds. He was doing well, and in his discharge sheets, she wrote the wonderful words: "No further follow-up examinations are required at this time." Maximus was healed!

Scarred but Whole Again

We saw Maximus again in August of 2018. I asked the owner to bring him in to get more details about her kitty both before and after the injury. Plus, we wanted to see how Maximus was doing. He looked like a different cat. He was bigger and had gained weight. His beautiful bushy white hair coat with those streaks of cream color on his face, ears, and trunk, and bright, clear light blue eyes were now on full display. It was the first time the doctors and technicians saw him with a full haircoat, and he looked terrific. He was affectionate with us and seemed happy to show off his healed body and sunny disposition.

Maximus re-wrote the book on an animal's ability to heal massive thermal burns on its body. I thought that a cat with 40 percent of his surface area burned would have no chance of survival. Maximus qualifies as one of the most incredible stories of healing that I know.

Several factors helped Maximus win his fight for survival. His owners sought veterinary help immediately after the injury. Any delay in his treatment would have made a bad situation even worse. His age was also a factor—at only six months old, he was barely full-grown and was in good physical condition before the injury. Studies have found that children can withstand a more extensive body area of burn injury and still survive compared to adults.[21] Maximus's youth may have also helped with another element in his recovery—his willingness to start eating just days after the injury. Imagine if you were Maximus, and your body was riddled with large, painful, open wounds with dead skin peeling off. Food would be the last thing you were interested in. Maximus somehow developed an appetite despite the pain and anxiety he was experiencing. Like many other animals we present in this book, his nutritional intake was key to his survival.

Finally, Maximus's happy ending was due to his medical care from his doctor (Becky), his owner, and the veterinary technicians at MedVet Toledo. Countless hours were spent dressing his wounds, giving him medications, keeping him clean, and helping him in and out of the litter box. Comforting him with petting, talking, and tender loving care was essential to his recovery. He received state-of-the-art veterinary medical care both at the hospital and at home. The owner treated Maximus as if he were one of her pediatric patients. The family's dedication to him was remarkable.

But just as with all the animals described in this book, Maximus himself was responsible for making his body whole again. In English, the name Maximus means "greatest." In healing and fighting through the suffering, he was the greatest. He persevered through horrible pain and disability. His story is significant to anyone, especially those who have suffered similar injuries and need inspiration. Maximus is a testimony to the ability of the living body to repair itself even in a dire clinical situation. All burn patients that we see from this point on will be compared to this beautiful cream and white cat with blue eyes and a remarkable spirit. Thank you, Maximus Quintus, for having the courage to endure and showing us the miracle of healing.

Chapter 9: Bruiser

I was so uncomfortable. The combination of the hot surgery lamp shining on my head, the heavy cloth surgical cap, mask, and gown, and my bundle of nerves had me sweating from head to toe. I reached into the dog's abdomen and tried to recognize what I was feeling. Somewhere in his belly was a spleen, and I had to find it. The organs were slippery and moist. It was impossible to hold anything. Everything slipped out of my hands when I tried to grab it. It was like trying to pull a fish out of a pond with your bare hands. I knew where the spleen was supposed to be from pictures in anatomy books. But this was a live dog, and I had never done a splenectomy before. I had never done any surgery at all. You see, I wasn't even a doctor.

I was a second-year veterinary student operating on a live dog. I had no business doing surgery on a real animal. I didn't know a scalpel from a retractor from a forceps. I was way out of my comfort zone, but the surgical laboratory course was a curriculum requirement. Each student had to operate on live animals to pass the course. With minimal training in instruments and handling the delicate tissues, we performed major surgical procedures on live dogs.

All veterinarians are expected to be surgeons. Routine surgical procedures such as spay, neuter, skin tumor removal, and repair of skin lacerations are considered part of everyday veterinary clinical practice. Even if they don't like surgery, veterinary students are obligated to take courses that teach them surgical principles and techniques. Knowledge of surgical instruments, suture materials, surgical anatomy, and surgical approaches to the various parts of the body are all required elements of the veterinary curriculum.

Equally important as the academic knowledge of surgery are the manual skills necessary to perform the procedures. Surgical skill is difficult to master, more so for some students than others. Some students love surgery, and developing the manual skills and using them on the patient is enjoyable. For others, the mere thought of laying a scalpel to the skin of a living creature transforms them into a chaotic mass of nerves and fear.

Today's veterinary colleges understand that fear and have developed well-organized, step-by-step methods to learn surgical skills. Students learn basic skills on tissue and organ models, building their confidence through repetitive practice and mastery of fundamental skills, such as tying a square knot and suturing layers of tissues. Once they complete those skills, they move on to laboratory sessions where, on canine cadavers, they learn more advanced techniques. Finally, under the supervision of the faculty, students in the teaching laboratories operate on live animals. They perform routine procedures such as spaying and neutering. These animals are usually dogs and cats from animal shelters or rescue organizations that are spayed or neutered before being adopted. The students, therefore, are performing beneficial surgery on animals who will recover and find homes. Future doctors, animal shelters, and the animals themselves benefit from this arrangement.

But these well-designed and executed training programs were unavailable forty-five years ago when I was a veterinary student. In our second year in the curriculum, we were thrust into the surgery laboratory to perform various procedures on live dogs. Some of them were advanced surgeries that we shouldn't have been doing.

In our second year of vet school, we were assigned a dog from the local pound to be our surgery dog for the entire course. These were homeless dogs that would eventually be euthanized because no one had adopted them. The current extensive network of humane societies and rescue organizations that find homes for stray or unwanted dogs did not yet exist when I was in veterinary school. Each week, our dog was put under general anesthesia and underwent a major operation under the supervision of our professors. Once completed, the dogs were stitched up, woken up from anesthesia, and placed back in their cages. The dogs received no further treatment after the lab—no antibiotics, no pain relievers, nothing except a bowl of dry kibble dog food and some water. We knew it was inhumane, but we had no choice in the matter. If you wanted to graduate from veterinary school, this was a necessary evil that had to be done.[24]

Friends from Day One

Even after many years, I still remember my surgery dog. I even saved a picture of us together. He was a handsome, medium-sized (about forty pounds) mixed breed male dog. His short hair coat was a mixture of different shades of brown, and he was about the size of an English spaniel. He was in good condition and had a wonderful personality. The first time I went to see him, he immediately stood up, wagged his tail frantically, and couldn't wait to jump out of his cage and get some attention. Considering what would happen, I probably should not have gotten attached to him, but I couldn't help it. We immediately became friends, and there was no going back.

The first surgical lab was scheduled for later in the week after we were assigned our dogs. The procedure to be performed was a splenectomy or removal of the spleen. Splenectomy is commonly performed on dogs, usually due to splenic cancer. Our dog's spleen was normal; it was being removed just so we could learn how to do it. I read the course handouts and whatever I could find in surgery textbooks to prepare for the lab. That wasn't easy since there were very few textbooks, and the available ones were not very good. There was no Internet with its wealth of information, including surgical photographs, videos, and step-by-step instructions on surgical techniques.

As the day of the lab approached, I started getting nervous. I would be doing surgery on my new lovable friend, which I'd never done before. There were three students in my lab group, including me. One would be responsible for anesthesia, I was the primary surgeon, and the other was the assistant surgeon. As the primary surgeon for this lab, all eyes would be on me.

The big day arrived, and the three of us met before the lab to talk about our plan. There was also an orientation session with the faculty member to discuss the technical aspects of the anesthesia and the surgical procedure. Once we had a pretty good idea what our respective jobs were, we brought our dog, who was still nameless, into the surgical laboratory room and started working on him. We put him on the surgical table and started the anesthesia. He wagged his tail the whole time; he was just so happy to have people touching him and paying attention to him. He first received an anesthetic drug that made him sleepy enough to pass an endotracheal tube into his trachea. The gas anesthesia was delivered through this tube. All of this went fine, and he was soon asleep so we could put him in the proper position on the table and prepare his abdomen for sterile surgery.

I was getting more nervous by the minute. Sure, I had read all about how to do a splenectomy, but what if something went wrong? The more I read about the anatomy the night before, the scarier it looked. The spleen is one of the most vascular organs in the body with many blood vessels and lots of possibilities for bleeding. The splenic artery and vein divide into fifty to sixty smaller blood vessels that supply the spleen with blood. All of them would have to be tied off and then severed to allow for removal of the organ. What if a ligature slipped, or I didn't tie it tight enough? What if the spleen fell apart while I tried to work on it? I was doing everything possible to hide my anxiety, but it was getting harder and harder as zero hour approached.

I put on my cap and mask and scrubbed in for the surgery. "Scrubbing" is the time-honored ritual of washing one's hands and arms with an antiseptic soap and scrub-brush to remove germs. I put on my sterile gown and gloves and got ready to begin the surgery. Besides having to wear all this uncomfortable clothing, I had to maintain aseptic technique or as they say, do not break sterility. One must not touch anything that isn't sterile, including my nose which now itched like crazy! All of this just added to my anxiety.

After placing sterile drapes around our canine "patient," I loaded a blade on the scalpel and readied it to make the initial incision in the skin. The scalpel is an oddly shaped instrument with an exquisitely sharp blade attached to the handle. Mastery of the scalpel is one of the first things a surgeon learns. It must be appropriately held, passed to other surgeons correctly, and placed on the skin carefully. The pressure necessary to cut the skin is only slightly more than infinitesimal. Less than adequate pressure would not cut the skin, requiring more attempts and causing too much trauma to the tissue. But too much pressure would not only cut the skin but the other layers below, possibly cutting into one of the abdominal organs.

I managed to cut the skin on the abdominal midline without too much embarrassment, although it did take me more than one swipe with the blade. The next step was to dissect through the subcutaneous tissue layer and find the linea alba. The linea alba, Latin for the "white line," is an elusive landmark where all the abdominal muscles come together on the exact midline of the belly. It's the ideal place to make the incision through the abdominal wall. But the surgeon must cut directly on it, otherwise, the blade will slice the abdominal muscle. The result will be a bloody, messy incision and likely a bad grade for the lab session. The linea alba can be hard to find, especially for a novice surgeon. After fumbling around for about half an hour, I finally found it, incised through it, and entered the dog's abdominal cavity. The sweat was already rolling down my back.

The abdomen of a dog, and all mammals for that matter, is a collection of major organs, blood vessels, and fatty membranes. It houses the liver, kidneys, stomach, countless feet of intestines, pancreas, urinary bladder, and other smaller structures such as the adrenal glands and lymph nodes. And, somewhere in this menagerie is the spleen, the organ that was currently playing a cruel game of hide and seek with me.

I placed my gloved hand inside—everything felt warm, soft, and squishy. The inexperienced surgeon is at once mystified and intimidated by the feeling of touching these delicate organs. How much manipulation could I do without harming or rupturing something, causing catastrophic bleeding and damage to the structure? When I found the spleen, how would I move it into a position where I could see it and properly work on it? And why was I suddenly feeling so hot and light-headed inside this cap, mask, and surgery gown?

I tried to calm down by focusing on the job at hand. The spleen is a long, thin, tongue-shaped, purplish organ in the abdomen attached to the cavity's interior by a sheet of fatty tissue containing a thousand blood vessels. Well, that number is, of course, an exaggeration, but that's how it seemed at the time. After several more minutes of the splenic reconnaissance effort, I finally found it. My goal was to lift it out of the abdomen without ripping or crushing it or its blood vessels. Then I could start dissecting, ligating, and severing those countless vessels. I spent a ridiculous amount of time getting the slimy spleen out of the belly. Because of the drugs we had given for anesthesia, the spleen was engorged with blood, making it about three to four times its normal size. Afraid the spleen would completely disintegrate in my hands, I tried gently coaxing it out of the abdomen. I hoped that somehow it would finally give up the struggle and agree to be liberated out of its safe confines in the deep recesses of the abdominal cavity.

Eventually I won the wrestling match. The spleen was sitting just outside the abdominal incision where I could work on it. I set it to one side of the incision. I examined the fantastic array of arteries and veins going in and out of the organ. The vessels look like small squiggly worms colored in various shades of red and purple. The arteries were throbbing with each beat of the heart, which of course, scared me to death. With instruments that seemed ill-suited for the task, I started to dissect out the vessels so they could be clamped, tied off with sutures, and severed. I was slow and tentative, being overly cautious to avoid any catastrophes. After about thirty minutes, I had ligated and cut only a fraction of the vessels—I was taking way too long. On top of that the student doing anesthesia on our dog became alarmed. "Hey, our dog is pale, and his heart rate is climbing!" he yelled. Something was not right with our patient; he was going into shock.

We called our lab instructor over to help us. The first thing he noticed was a large pool of blood on the floor below our surgery table. We traced the stream of blood to the very end of the spleen. When I had pulled the spleen out of the abdomen, I had torn it, allowing a lot of blood to flow out of it. The instructor told us our dog needed intravenous fluids for the shock and that I needed to ligate the rest of those splenic blood vessels immediately to stop the hemorrhaging.

Then something unexpected happened—instead of succumbing to the pressure and having a complete panic-stricken meltdown, I became robotic. I took the hemostats, gave the scissors to my assistant, and began quickly and methodically dissecting, ligating, and cutting the rest of the splenic blood vessels. I finished them in about fifteen minutes. We removed the spleen from the abdomen, placed it on the instrument table, and began closing the abdominal incision. In the meantime, the anesthesia student ran intravenous fluids to our dog quickly to raise his blood pressure and get him out of shock. His vital signs promptly improved. I finished closing the incision, but it took longer than it should have, again because of my clumsiness and lack of experience. We took our dog off the anesthetic gas, and soon he started to wake up. He was going to live. I quietly thanked God for allowing my first surgical case to survive despite my incompetence.

We got him bedded down in his cage, and I stayed with him for several hours until he was fully awake and his vital signs were stable. The next day I checked on him first thing in the morning before our classes started, and found him standing up, wagging his tail. What a trooper. Less than 24 hours earlier, the handsome guy had been near death. Now he was not only alive, but wagging his tail, eating, and licking my face. His incision looked okay, but there was some bruising. From that day on, I gave him the name Bruiser. It was just the first of many bruises he would have.

The Weekly Ritual

Each week a different surgery was performed on Bruiser. The procedures were those commonly performed by veterinarians in private practice: incision into the stomach, opening the urinary bladder, and castration were just some of the surgeries Bruiser endured. My surgery skills gradually improved, which at least to some degree was helpful to him since I was causing less trauma.

The morning after each surgery, there he would be standing in his cage, excited to see me. Because I felt bad for him, each week I would swing by the grocery store on my way to school to get him some canned food. I wanted him to have something a little tastier to eat than the cheap, dry kibble available in the kennel. After eating his breakfast, I would take him outside to lie in the sunshine. Something inside me thought that not only was the sun, fresh air, and petting good for his psyche, but it could also help his incisions heal faster. Clinical studies have found that to be true.[13] Even Florence Nightingale, the famous pioneering nurse who devoted her life to treating the sick, knew that patients recover from illness faster if they are exposed to sunshine. People or animals who are emotionally supported, well cared for, given therapeutic massage (or petting in animals) heal their wounds and recover from illness faster than those that are not.[25] I don't know how much the little things I did for Bruiser helped him, but it made me feel better, and he seemed to like it.

I don't remember exactly how many surgeries we did on Bruiser; I think it was about seven or eight procedures. The second to last surgery we did was the most painful for him. After placing him under anesthesia, we made a surgical approach to his femur (thigh bone). I made a long incision in the skin and subcutaneous tissues of the thigh. The muscles were retracted to expose the middle of the bone. We sawed the femur in half using a bone-cutting instrument composed of multiple sharp wires. Essentially, we created a mid-shaft femoral fracture. We then repaired the fracture using an intramedullary bone pin. These are variably sized, solid stainless-steel rods with a trocar point on each end. To place the pin, one connects it to a pin chuck, or handle, which allows the pin to be driven into the bone. I drove the rod, by hand, into the medullary canal of the bone, the central longitudinal space within the bone where the bone marrow is located. The two ends of the fractured bone are put back into alignment, and the pin is driven down into the lower segment of the femur. In this way, the pin spans the fractured bone and stabilizes it, theoretically allowing it to heal.

If you have ever had a broken bone, you know how intensely painful it is. The pain comes from a thin membrane surrounding the bone called the periosteum, which has many nerve endings, making it very sensitive to manipulation and injury. When I went to see Bruiser the next day, he greeted me as usual, immediately standing up and wagging his tail. But he was holding his leg up and not putting any weight on it. Of course, the thigh was swollen and had some bruising along the incision. That's convincing evidence that his leg hurt badly, and why not—we had just stripped the bone of its tissue attachments, broken it, and placed a metal rod inside of it.

Bruiser got two cans of delicious dog food that morning. I felt so bad for him. How could he still be wagging his tail and be friendly toward me? Dogs both love unconditionally and forgive unconditionally. I know the skeptics will say that dogs can't understand the source of their discomfort and therefore wouldn't associate me with the pain, but the forgiveness was still real to me. His willingness to remain my friend throughout those several weeks of pain almost made it worse; he didn't deserve what was happening to him, but he didn't blame anyone. He just accepted his situation and made the best of it. When he ravenously ate the canned food, he looked like he was the happiest dog in the world. He was such a good dog and a good friend.

Each day of the week after the fracture surgery, Bruiser started putting more and more weight on the leg. But he was still noticeably lame. Fractures take several weeks to heal, and until the healing is complete, there will be some degree of lameness and discomfort. But the thigh swelling started to go down, and he seemed to be in less pain. His other incisions were healing well, and gradually I could take out some of his stitches. He had been shaved in so many places he was almost completely bald.

A Sad Farewell

Then it was Bruiser's last week to have surgery performed, which of course, was good news for him, but there was a catch. After this final surgery, we had to euthanize him. His ordeal would be over, and I was glad for that, but I would lose my friend, who had been so cooperative and brave over the past several weeks. Saying that I had mixed emotions would be putting it mildly.

The last surgical procedure was a thoracotomy. We would be opening the chest cavity through an incision between two ribs. We were instructed to explore the cavity and examine the lungs, major blood vessels, and the beating heart. All very exciting, but my enthusiasm was tempered by what had to be done at the end.

Before putting him under anesthesia, I said goodbye to him. I thanked him for all he had done for me, and I said I was sorry for causing him all that pain. He just looked at me with trusting eyes and licked my face. We gave him the anesthetic drugs, placed him in the proper position on the surgery table, and began the procedure.

A lateral thoracotomy allows the surgeon to enter the thoracic cavity through a series of incisions in the muscles between the ribs. The thorax is a negative pressure cavity, one of the few places in the body where a vacuum is found. The negative pressure is essential in this part of the body, and without it, normal breathing would not be possible. Once the cavity is opened, this negative pressure is lost. The anesthetist must breathe for the animal using the anesthesia machine connected to the endotracheal tube.

Venturing inside the thorax is a unique experience for a surgeon. Whereas the abdominal cavity is a quiet place full of organs showing little visible activity, the thorax exudes life itself. Things are moving, beating, expanding, and contracting. The air-filled lungs, spongy, soft, and pink, grow large during inspiration, small on expiration. The heart is a giant muscle that alternately contracts, relaxes, and contracts again. Large pipes connect to the heart; they are the central blood vessels, the major highways of the circulatory system. Inside the thorax, one gets the sense it is the body's headquarters. So much important stuff goes on there. Every time I have surgically entered the chest cavity I get the feeling of being in the presence of one of nature's most profound systems. I feel privileged to observe the beating heart, the breathing lungs, and pulsing vessels. One must respect these vital and sensitive machines. The skilled surgeon treads lightly in the thorax; it is not a place to be careless or heavy-handed.

My excitement in experiencing Bruiser's internal thoracic structures was, as I said before, tempered by knowing what had to be done when the surgery was completed. After placing the final stitch in his skin and while under anesthesia, we gave him the euthanasia drugs until his heart stopped beating. Just like that, our saga together was over. We wouldn't be moving him back to his cage tonight, my errand to the grocery store for some canned food no longer necessary.

All the surgery groups put their dead dogs in black bags and then placed them in a large container. The bodies would be taken to a rendering plant and processed, not a very dignified funeral for these creatures who had sacrificed so much. Many of us wished we could have adopted our surgery dogs, and I would have done so in a heartbeat. But the faculty told us it was forbidden due to regulations about laboratory animals used in the university. We were aware of that from the beginning of the course, but it didn't prevent us from getting attached to them. How could we not get attached to them?

Stephen Birchard

He Gave His Life for Me

Bruiser gave his life for me to learn how to be a doctor and a surgeon. He gave his body for me to clip, shave, inject, incise, dissect, and suture repeatedly. He helped me learn surgical instruments, techniques, and sutures. He showed me how tissues heal and become functional again, how blood loss from an unknown tear in the spleen can cause shock, and how painful a fractured bone can be. I gained confidence in my abilities because of him, which would ultimately lead me to a lifelong career in surgery.

All this Bruiser did while seeking no reward, gratitude, or consolation. All he wanted from me was some affection, a delicious can of food once a week, and a little time in the sun. I wish there had been some way I could have repaid him for his service to me. We had a mutual bond, but let's face it, I received much more from him than I could ever give back. I wonder if it would help him to know that thousands of sick and injured animals, including all the animals in this book, have benefited from his sacrifice. He was a handsome mixed breed dog who, despite week after week of pain and suffering, greeted me with a wagging tail and a lick on my face. I will never forget my friend and teacher, Bruiser the dog.

Chapter 10: Tigger

"Dr. Birchard, would you mind looking at a cat we just admitted to the hospital? He's having trouble breathing."

"Sure," I said, following the veterinary student to the cat's cage in the orthopedic ward. "Tell me about him. What's his history?" I asked.

"This is Tigger, a six-month-old male neutered cat who was hit by a car a few days ago. The owner's local veterinarian examined him. He found that Tigger had a fractured thigh bone of the left rear leg. He referred Tigger to us for the repair of the fracture. I thought he was fine otherwise, but after putting him in his cage, I watched him for a while, and I think his breathing is abnormal. It's fast, and he seems to be working harder to breathe than he should. At first, I thought he was just excited about being here, but he's still doing it after settling down. I'm pretty concerned about him."

"Did you listen to him with your stethoscope?" I asked.

"Yes," she said, "and his lungs sound fine. What do you think? Is it something serious?"

"Let's have a look," I said.

The Ohio State veterinary student was right to be concerned. Although sitting quietly in his cage, Tigger was breathing faster than normal, considering he was resting. He was also expanding his chest wider than a healthy cat would do. But he wasn't in severe distress. When I opened the cage to examine him closer, he started purring. I listened to him with my stethoscope, and like the student, I didn't hear anything concerning; the heart and lungs sounded fine, and his gum color was pink.

I told the student I agreed with her assessment that Tigger was showing signs of being mildly dyspneic, the medical term for having trouble breathing. "What do you think we should do?" I asked her. "I would get chest films on him," she said. I agreed.

Radiographs of his chest would help us determine the cause of his abnormal breathing. After the kind of trauma he had suffered, there were many possibilities for internal damage that could have occurred. Lung bruising, lung rupture, or internal bleeding are common after being hit by a car. "Let's see if the radiology folks can get them right away," I said.

I walked down to the Radiology Department to tell them about Tigger and requested x-rays of his chest. I asked the radiology students and technicians to be gentle with him since he had a fracture, and we were concerned about his breathing. Having x-rays taken is not painful, but being handled by strangers can be stressful for any animal, let alone an injured one. They thanked me for the information and promised to obtain the films soon.

An X-ray Picture is Worth a Thousand Words

Once the radiographs were finished, I put the films on the lighted view box. (This was before digital radiography.) At first, I didn't see any significant problems. The lungs were fully inflated and appeared normal, the heart was fine, and there were no rib fractures. But as I continued to examine the images, I started finding some issues. He had pneumomediastinum, or free air in the middle of the chest that contains the windpipe, major blood vessels, and the esophagus. The only air in the chest cavity should be in the lungs, not floating freely in the cavity. Rupture of the trachea (windpipe), bronchus, or esophagus could cause the issue I saw on the films. Looking more carefully at the trachea, I saw what looked like an air-filled bubble in the middle of it between the neck and the heart. I hadn't seen anything like it before, so I asked one of the radiologists for their opinion. As all good radiologists do, she carefully examined all the images entirely before offering her observations. I tried to be patient but couldn't wait to hear what she thought.

"Interesting," she said. "He has pneumomediastinum," (*Okay, good, she agrees with me on that part!*) "and I think I see where the free air is coming from."

"Where?" I asked anxiously.

"Well, I can follow the trachea down from his neck, then there is about a one-inch gap, then I see the trachea again closer to the heart."

"Are you telling me he has a complete rupture of the trachea, and the two ends are one inch apart?" I asked.

"Yes," she replied. "And the only thing connecting the two ends are the thin membranes of the mediastinum." It took me a minute to digest this information—she had just described a potentially life-threatening injury for Tigger.

Think of the respiratory system as a tree. The lungs are the leaves, the bronchi are the branches, and the trachea is the trunk. All air going to the lungs gets there via the trachea. It is the pipeline for the oxygen that animals, including us, need to live. Tigger's was broken. When he·was hit by the car, the trachea separated, leaving the ends one inch apart from each other. My first thought was: How can he get air past that gap and into the lungs? My second thought was: How is he still alive?

The student and I carefully took Tigger back to his cage. He remained surprisingly stable, but knowing what was wrong made us especially gentle with him. We stayed with him for a few minutes to ensure his breathing did not worsen. He settled down and even ate a little food. I transferred him to the ICU to be monitored and receive medication to relieve pain. Then I called Tigger's owners to update them on our findings.

I told the owners that Tigger was stable, but we had found a serious problem. In addition to his fractured leg, he had a ruptured trachea, an unusual injury that needed to be corrected surgically. But it would be difficult, and he could die during the procedure. It also would be expensive. The owners expressed surprise and confusion. "We thought he only had a broken bone in his leg," they said anxiously. I explained how we'd noticed some mild breathing issues when he was admitted to the hospital, and that radiographs demonstrated the ruptured trachea. After a few questions and more discussion, they approved to surgically fix both the trachea and his leg. I thanked them and said I would keep them updated.

Developing a Plan of Action

Since Tigger was stable and would be watched all night by the ICU staff, I scheduled his surgery for the following day. This would allow me to discuss his case with the anesthesiologist and develop a plan. General anesthesia, where the patient is completely asleep, involves breathing an anesthetic gas through a small tube placed inside the trachea. Oxygen is also given through this tube during the anesthesia. In Tigger, this would be difficult since the trachea was ruptured. How could we be sure the oxygen and gas would travel across the ruptured area and enter the lungs? What would prevent him from developing low blood oxygen and rapidly dying during the anesthesia? We had entered uncharted territory with Tigger. Honestly, I wasn't sure it would be possible to fix this friendly little cat.

The anesthesia faculty and I decided on Tigger's anesthesia and surgery plan. It would require coordinating our activities and good communication between the doctors working on him. Before finishing up my clinical duties for the day, my students and I did ward rounds, which included discussing the plan for Tigger. Then we checked on Tigger to be sure he was doing okay. He was curled up in the back of his cage, looking comfortable, so I didn't bother him too much other than checking his vital signs. His breathing had not worsened and was even a little slower and less labored than it had been earlier. I was amazed that he looked so good, considering the problem with his trachea. He even purred some more: apparently, cats can purr with a ruptured trachea. I scratched his head and gently petted him before leaving the ICU.

Sleep didn't come easily for me that night. I had never done surgery like this before. I kept going over in my head how I would perform the operation. I thought of some instruments I would need to do the surgery and wrote them down to give to the surgical technician in the morning. I wanted everything to go well. Tigger was an affectionate and handsome little cat, and his owners loved him dearly. I was eager to face the challenges but anxious about the risks.

Fixing the Oxygen Pipeline

The following day, the students and I did ward rounds. I hadn't received any calls about Tigger from ICU overnight, so I assumed he was doing fine. My student assigned to him had already looked him over and updated his status. She said he seemed fine, although still breathing slightly faster than usual. His heart and lungs sounded fine, and although he had pain in his fractured leg, he was resting comfortably.

She had already updated the owners on his condition.

I had other patients scheduled for surgery that day. I put Tigger first on the list so that when his operation was finished we could monitor him during the day while the hospital was fully staffed. I preferred to do the complicated procedures first when I was the most rested and clear-headed. (After tossing and turning for a while the night before, I finally did get some sleep.) I met with the anesthesiologists briefly again to review our plan and told them we were ready to start. After moving Tigger to the preoperative prep area where the surgical patients are anesthetized and prepared for surgery, we clipped his hair. We scrubbed the skin over the right side of his chest, where we would be making the incision to enter his thorax. Typically, this clipping and cleaning of the surgical site are done when the animal is under anesthesia, but we wanted to begin Tigger's surgery as soon as he was anesthetized.

The anesthetist placed an intravenous catheter in Tigger's front leg and injected the anesthetic drugs. Once he was asleep, an endotracheal tube was gently placed by opening his mouth and using an oral speculum to guide the tube through his throat and into the trachea. These tubes come in various sizes, and one is usually chosen to match the size of the animal's trachea. In Tigger, we used a smaller one than usual to prevent more injury. The anesthetist was also careful not to use the anesthesia machine to force air into the lungs through the tube. Usually, this is done intermittently, but in Tigger, it could cause the very tenuous connection between the ends of the trachea to break down. This would have been catastrophic because then no air could get into the lungs.

The technicians quickly moved Tigger into the operating room and positioned him on the table for the surgery. My assistants and I were already scrubbed and in caps, masks, and sterile gowns, waiting for him to arrive. We placed the surgical drapes on him while the anesthetist quickly connected Tigger to an EKG and other vital sign monitors—time was of the essence. Things were going well, but everyone was on edge.

The surgical approach we used is called a right lateral thoracotomy. We made an incision on the right side of Tigger's chest from the top of his body to the bottom near his sternum. The skin, subcutaneous tissue, and muscle layers between the ribs were all incised with a scalpel or surgical scissors. When the chest cavity was open, I placed a retractor to spread Tigger's ribs apart so I could see the trachea. Within a few minutes of entering his chest, I noticed that Tigger's body tissues had turned a bluish-gray color. Blood oozing out of the muscle became a very dark reddish-purple, not the usual red ketchup color. The anesthetist nervously said, "Dr. Birchard, Tigger's blood oxygen level is rapidly decreasing! His lungs are collapsed; no air is getting in them!"

I needed to work faster. Without adequate oxygen, Tigger could suffer brain damage, go into cardiac arrest, and die within minutes. My hands became sweaty and trembled slightly. I asked my assistant to grab a retractor. "Move the lungs away from the trachea so I can see," I said. I heard the clock ticking—how long could Tigger go without oxygen? With some quick but careful dissection of the tissues around the trachea, I found the end of it. I saw the tip of the endotracheal tube that the anesthetist had passed. I grabbed it with forceps, pulled it farther out, and inserted it into the downstream tracheal segment (the part connected to the bronchi and lungs). The tube provided a pathway for the air and oxygen to get into the lungs.

"The endotracheal tube is now across the defect in the trachea!" I quickly told the anesthetist. "You can start ventilating him!" The anesthetist began to push air through the tube using the Ambu (ambulatory) bag. The lungs began expanding. Tigger's color improved, and his blood oxygen level quickly went back up to normal. Now we could slow down, take a deep breath, and begin repairing the trachea.

When an animal's thoracic cavity is surgically opened, the lungs cannot function. Air pressure inside the thorax is negative or below atmospheric pressure. The ribs are pulled out during inhalation, expanding the lungs and creating negative pressure inside the trachea. Air is pulled into the trachea, bronchi, and lungs. The lungs do not inflate during inhalation when the chest cavity is open, and negative pressure cannot be generated. Forcing air under pressure into the trachea using either the Ambu-bag connected to the anesthesia machine or a mechanical ventilator overcomes that issue. On Tigger we couldn't do that until I got the endotracheal tube past the tracheal defect.

I had my assistants place more retractors so I could see all the damaged areas. As we suspected from the chest films, there was a complete separation of the trachea, and the two ends were about one inch apart. It was as if something had just cut the trachea in half, leaving the ends dangling in space. Thankfully, the tissues looked healthy, so I didn't have to remove any tracheal tissue, which would have made the repair more difficult. I began the tedious job of sewing the two ends back together using sutures. The trachea in a cat is small, about the size of a pencil. To be sure that each suture was properly placed in the tracheal wall, I had to pre-place the sutures. This means placing them all first without tying them, then tying them one by one to complete the tracheal repair. I finished the suturing, but before closing the chest incision, I asked the anesthetist to gently move the endotracheal tube back and forth. I wanted to ensure that none of my sutures had penetrated the tube and inadvertently anchored it inside the trachea. Now was the time to discover that, not when the surgery was over when we were trying to pull the endotracheal tube out of Tigger's throat.

After we finished our part of Tigger's surgery, the orthopedic team came in and fixed his fractured femur. The orthopedic surgeon placed a pin inside the bone to stabilize it. That surgery went well, and Tigger's vital signs remained stable during the remainder of his anesthesia.

Tigger was moved to the recovery area and closely monitored by the anesthesia staff when all the surgeries were completed. The endotracheal tube was carefully removed when he was awake enough to breathe without it. It slid out smoothly, and Tigger continued to breathe without problems. He was moved back to his cage in the ICU for continued monitoring of vital signs. I called the owners to let them know the surgery was completed, and he was doing well so far. They were ecstatic, but I warned them that he wasn't out of the woods just yet. We would have to see how he did over the next few days.

I still had several surgeries to perform that day, but I wanted to check on Tigger every chance I got. I was worried about him. I hoped that the brief period of hypoxia had not caused brain damage or injury to other organs. I couldn't wait for him to wake up so I could assess him neurologically. After I finished my second surgery of the day, I walked down to the

ICU. I could see his cage from a distance. He was standing up, looking around.

I opened his cage door to examine him. He looked great! His vision was fine (hypoxia to the brain can cause blindness), his heart and lungs sounded good, and his gums were pink. Although a little sleepy, he quickly regained his affectionate behavior, rubbing his head on the cage door seeking attention. He loved being petted and started eating small amounts of canned cat food later in the afternoon—what a tough little kitty. I had only known him for twenty-four hours, but I liked him a lot.

Breathing Easier (Tigger, and Us!)

Tigger had an uneventful night in ICU, and by the morning, he looked fantastic. I was tempted to send him home but told the owners we'd better keep him confined to a cage for one more day. We obtained radiographs of his chest, which looked good—it was amazing how much better the trachea looked on x-ray films once it was put back together. He went home the next day to owners overwhelmed with joy to get him back. The student gave them their discharge instructions, which included strict orders to keep him confined indoors and rest for one month. It's not easy to enforce rest on a cat, but they said they would do the best they could.

Tigger returned to Ohio State a month after the surgery for a recheck examination. His local veterinarian had taken out the skin stitches two weeks postoperatively, and the incision was healed. He was acting completely normal, and his heart and lungs sounded good. We repeated the chest films, which were normal. You could see a very slight indentation of the trachea where it had been repaired, but otherwise it looked great. He went back home with instructions to see his regular veterinarian in one month to assess the healing of his fracture.

I learned a lot from Tigger. I had no idea an animal could survive the kind of tracheal injury he had suffered, let alone be only mildly symptomatic. He reminded me of why we teach veterinary students to always obtain radiographs of the chest on animals that have been hit by cars. I was very impressed with the student who had noticed that Tigger was having trouble and knew what the next step should be. I think she got an "A" for that clinical rotation.

When he presented to us, no clinical studies had been published on Tigger's injury. We had no guidelines on how to treat tracheal avulsion in cats. We had to rely on basic physiology and common sense to work things out. Since then, papers have been published describing this injury in several cats and the treatment results.[26]

Tigger reminded me of the importance of having a preoperative plan to fix a life-threatening problem. We don't always have the luxury of planning our treatment on emergency cases. The animal must often be taken to surgery immediately without much consultation between specialists. But Tigger was only mildly symptomatic for his injury, giving us some time to prepare everything. The anesthesiologists did a fantastic job keeping Tigger alive during the operation. I was so glad it went well; Tigger had quickly found his way into my heart, and I desperately wanted to see him recover and go home to live a long and happy life. I hope he had many years of love and compassion with his dedicated family. He deserved it.

Chapter 11: Trust the Wagging Tail

With each thump of his tail, Rip said to me: "I'm not ready to die." All the animals in this book had a very severe disease or injury that, from a strictly medical standpoint, should have resulted in death. I am not exaggerating. I have seen hundreds of animals with lesser afflictions succumb to their illnesses. Although hard to pinpoint, something in these animals allowed them to overcome horrible injury or disease, even when it seemed hopeless. I have attempted to offer my own opinion into their power to get them through their suffering. But I also defer to you, the reader of these stories, to offer your own insight into these extraordinary creatures. How do you think they were able to persevere and win the battle for healing and survival?

These animal survivors changed my professional and personal life, helping me become a better doctor and a better person. Because of them, I learned new medical and surgical principles and techniques, gained confidence, and was reminded that "where there's life, there's hope." I also learned to stay hopeful like Rip, persevere like Bob, love life like Billy Bob, withstand pain like Maximus, forgive like Charlie, and be generous like Bruiser. Good doctors never stop being students, and I was fortunate to have patients who helped me on the journey of life-long learning.

Thump, Thump, Thump

In each case, there were times when the animal's medical status appeared too hopeless to continue. How could Rip sustain four major surgeries in a few months? How could Charlie and Maximus ever heal their broken bodies and be able to function? How long would Billy Bob live after the first cancer operation on her nose? Was it only a matter of time before Hershey's infection would spread to her bloodstream? And how could we possibly extract the arrow from Josie's heart without her dying of massive bleeding? All these worst-case scenarios were carefully considered and, in some cases, nearly led to a decision to euthanize. Yet, in each patient, something told us not to give up hope because the energy and the spirit of life, however precarious, continued to flow through their bodies. Like Rip's slow but steady tail wag when his illness was so bad it was the only part of his body he could move, there was at least that feeble sign that he wasn't giving up. No matter your connection to a critically sick or injured animal, watch for a sign that they are trying to tell you not to lose hope. Because if you decide not to give up, the dog or cat will know it, and they will keep on fighting.

Those caring for people with life-threatening or even terminal illnesses may have similar experiences. Seriously ill people may not have a tail to wag, but they can send messages that they want to continue the fight for life. Caregivers can assure them that they will be by their side; they don't have to struggle alone. The gift of being there to take the journey with them is one of the most meaningful things we can do for our loved ones when illness strikes.

Skill and Will: What Doctor and Patient Bring to the Healing Process

Treatment of the animals in this book required the combination of a skilled team of professionals, excellent facilities, and committed owners. Although the medical treatment of these patients was crucial, some intangible factors also contributed to their healing, such as the will to live, the support and love from family members, and the animals' innate affectionate personality that drew people to them. As doctors, we are trained to be scientific in our methods, always striving for objectivity to make rational decisions. "Evidence-based medicine" is the goal—that is, to make treatment decisions based on the results of clinical research rather than just using intuition or personal experience. But striving to be purely objective makes it hard to discuss the forces of healing that go beyond the drugs, bandages, and surgeries. Healing "energy," "will to live," and "positive thinking" are difficult to quantify and analyze statistically. But I believe these abstract forces are critically important. A growing body of medical research validates this in humans and animals alike. Surrounding patients with love and support during their illness helps make them better.

This shouldn't be surprising to us. The body is a miraculous combination of physiologic processes and mechanisms; when they are in balance, the body is healthy. When injured, imbalanced, or stressed, the body's immune system is compromised, making the animal more susceptible to disease and injury. Touching animals—petting, scratching, and massaging not only makes them feel good; it brings them into a more balanced physiologic state that allows the body to heal its wounds, repair damaged organs, and fight infection. As a side effect, the caregiver benefits from this physical bond with the animal. Caring for pets supports us emotionally and physically, in a mutually beneficial relationship.

Cancer Takes Everything Except Our Love

Cancer is a strange and sinister illness. Unlike infections where germs invade the body from the outside, cancer is an insidious malfunction of the body's building blocks, the cells. The cancer cells revert to their biological origins, becoming immature and less differentiated. They multiply out of control and selfishly usurp the body of its nutrition, circulation, immune defenses, and energy. But, although cancer consumes everything, it can't destroy our love. Like Jack, Bob, and Billy Bob, we can still love and be loved, even when fighting the battle against cancer. If Bruce and Becky were asked if they had any regrets in doing so much to prolong the lives of their cherished friends with cancer, I think the answer would be an emphatic no. They joined their dogs in the fight for life and strengthened their already intense connection in the process. Cancer slowly drained the life out of Billy and Bob, but they could still love. Maybe that's what sustained them and allowed many years of quality time with their families.

Animals Can Have a Purpose-driven Life

Many of the animals we describe in this book had a larger purpose to their lives than simply being a pet, although that's an important purpose by itself. Rip was a professional athlete, Billy Bob was a medical service dog, Bruiser was my surgery laboratory dog, and Bob was my wife's constant companion, helping her through the ups and downs of her Army career and intense veterinary surgical training. Charlie's recovery from injury gave a gift of redemption to his owners, who were gripped by guilt and remorse. And the others, Josie, Hershey, and Maximus, were more than pets to their owners—they were members of their family who provided unconditional love and helped their owners sustain the stresses and strains of daily life. I would like to think that these pets knew they were needed, giving them additional motivation to fight through their suffering so that they could go on serving their critical function in their family's lives.

By telling these stories, I hope these animals can serve another purpose, one that they may not understand but could be the most important of all. An owner of a pet with cancer, or even someone who themselves has cancer, might look to Bob, Billy Bob, and Jack for encouragement to keep up the fight. Maximus might inspire a burn victim to help endure the pain and disability. Someone severely injured in an accident could say, "If Charlie can survive his gruesome wounds, then so can I." These animals collectively can speak to all of us, telling us that no matter how bleak things may look, there is always a glimmer of hope. If we can embrace that hope, maybe we can overcome our challenges, like Rip, Billy Bob, Charlie, Bruiser, Hershey, Bob, Josie, Maximus, Jack, and Tigger. Surviving allows us to give back some of the love and support that got us through the suffering. Maybe that is the ultimate lesson learned from injured animals. Even if we haven't experienced the same kind of medical problems they have, how can we not be in awe of their resilience? They will always inspire me to be a better doctor and person. I feel privileged to have participated in their care and become part of their lives.

Forgiveness

Sometimes we hurt the ones we love. It may not be intentional, but it hurts just the same. I have been on both sides of pain caused by loved ones—the one hurt, and the one inflicting the pain. I've learned that forgiveness opens the door to emotional healing. I forgave my father for being an abusive alcoholic, and my children forgave me for divorcing their mom. The paths to repairing these injured relationships were immensely difficult to navigate, but the starting point was forgiveness. Charlie forgave his owners for their mistake that broke his body. Some will argue that a dog is not intelligent enough to make that kind of decision, but the mere fact that he didn't appear to blame them or hold a grudge, is enough for me to believe that he forgave them. Dogs are sensitive to our moods, searching our faces for clues to our demeanor, and they can detect the smells our bodies emit when we are stressed. Charlie likely detected his family's worry and stress when they visited him. He responded to them with tail wagging and seeking their affection. In this way, as his physical wounds were healing, he was healing their emotional wounds with his love. Charlie reminded all of us about the power of forgiveness and love.

Believe in Yourself

A day in the life of a veterinarian, like all doctors, is filled with making decisions: assessing patients, choosing diagnostic tests, and sorting out treatment options, just to name a few. The ability to make decisions, whether it's as simple as the selection of a drug or as complex as how to remove an arrow from a beating heart, requires a basic but essential quality —believing in yourself. Without that, the doctor becomes paralyzed and ultimately ineffective.

Bruiser gave me my first chance to have faith in my abilities. When I nearly killed him by being too rough with his spleen and causing it to rupture and bleed, I had the choice to either panic or do what needed to be done. I don't think it's an exaggeration to say that I became a doctor that day. Somehow, I flipped an internal switch that allowed me to stay calm, overcome my fear of failure, and perform the splenectomy. Bruiser also started me on the path to becoming a surgical specialist, a daunting path in many respects. Complicated procedures like the ones described in these chapters require specialized training in a surgical residency program at either a college of veterinary medicine or specialty veterinary hospital, just like training programs for physicians who want to be surgeons. Programs to be specialists in surgery add four years of training after graduation from vet school and are intense and demanding learning experiences.

Josie provided another test of my confidence and ability to think on my feet. After opening her chest, I stared at the arrow that had skewered her heart. My hands, which are normally responsive to my directions, seemed to have developed a mind of their own and trembled uncontrollably. Even though surrounded by student assistants, I felt alone and a little helpless. The same calming energy that saved Bruiser flowed through me again to perform a surgery on Josie that was difficult and risky.

Many people think that surgeons are over-confident and cocky. Nothing could be further from the truth. As human as anyone else, we can be just as scared, nervous, and anxious as the next person. We overcome those feelings by knowing our patient, preparing for the surgical procedures by reviewing anatomy and technique, and operating in a meticulous, thorough, and deliberate fashion. Confidence doesn't just happen; you must work on it.

Final Thoughts

All the animals in this book, except of course for Bruiser, lived for years after recovering from their illness or injury. At the time of this writing, Hershey, Maximus, and Josie are still alive and doing well. Their owners were thrilled to get their beloved pet home, and none had any regrets about continuing treatment even when things looked hopeless. I imagine that all the animals in this book were spoiled rotten after their medical ordeal, as they should have been. The medical crisis no doubt intensified the already strong bond between pet and family.

The owners of the pets described in these stories had the financial resources to pay for the treatment of their animal companions. But the costs involved may have been beyond what some people could afford. This creates an unfortunate dynamic within the veterinary profession—we have made tremendous progress in our ability to diagnose and treat complicated and life-threatening diseases, but in some cases we have outpaced owners' ability to pay for it. Digital radiography, ultrasound, CT, and MRI imaging provide wonderful opportunities for diagnosis, but the equipment is expensive, and the cost to owners is high. Surgeries such as fracture repair, ligament reconstruction, thoracic surgery, neurosurgery, and microsurgery require expertise and expensive surgical equipment like that used in human medicine. As a result, these procedures are costly and beyond the reach of some pet caregivers, making them feel guilty and frustrated that they cannot give their pets the care they need. Veterinarians must be sensitive to these situations and offer less expensive options for treatment if available. Euthanasia may need to be considered if the pet's suffering is extreme and the prognosis without the expensive treatment is poor. This kind of decision-making requires the doctor to be compassionate in their communication and counseling of the distraught owners. It also takes an emotional toll on the veterinarian who desperately wants to safe the animal's life.

Medical insurance for pets is a growing industry and helps owners avoid the high cost of treating the kind of illnesses and injuries described in this book. Insurance could help solve the issue of the increasing cost of veterinary care. Since only a small percentage of our clients have pet health insurance, we need to educate owners about the advantages of having a policy for their animal family members. I have worked as a consultant for Trupanion, one of the many pet insurance companies available, and have been impressed with the service they provide.

I have presented many of the case studies in this book to veterinarians at continuing education seminars. I want as many people as possible to benefit from the experience of working with these wonderful creatures. I love to tell their stories, not to marvel at them as medical success stories, but to illustrate the power of the living body to heal. When a sick animal becomes healthy again, we celebrate for the sake of the animal and its owner and give them the credit. For they were the ones who suffered, both physically and emotionally, and they were the ones who overcame the odds and lived to tell their tale.

In my role as a teacher, I would repeatedly tell young veterinary students that the knowledge they gain in vet school is just the beginning of a lifelong journey of learning. Like my experience with the animals in this book, almost every day they will witness something new that they were not taught in school. They must be open to these experiences, remembering them and reflecting on them and comparing this experiential knowledge to what they have learned at the university or from textbooks and journals. Then they can use this knowledge, along with a healthy dose of common sense, to think like a doctor.

Each of the pets in this book taught me something new, something I didn't think possible. Each one reminded me that, even after over forty years as a vet, I still have a lot to learn, and I should not be quick to give up or be fatalistic. I am grateful for the opportunity to have participated in their medical care, and for the role they played in enhancing my professional and personal life. They will forever be etched in my mind. They inspired me with their fight for survival, and I am in awe of their courage. They touched me deeply, and I hope their stories have touched you as well.

Epilogue

Physician (Veterinarian), Heal Thyself

Life as a veterinarian can be difficult. We are expected to diagnose and cure diseases of creatures who cannot talk to us and in some cases forbid us to even touch them. We depend on owners of sick pets to give us a clear, relevant history of the animal's clinical signs and overall health issues. Because their pet is sick, these caregivers can be stressed, upset, and emotional. They want everything possible done for their cherished friend but may not be able to afford the treatment. Fear and frustration can lead to anger, which may then be transferred to the veterinarian, making the doctor-owner relationship unhealthy. Social media provides easy avenues for owners to vent their animosity, using language that can be disturbing and hurtful. Some vets find it difficult to cope with the emotional stress and strain caused by disgruntled clients. They may become depressed and even consider suicide, a growing problem in the profession.

Specialists in veterinary surgery are not exempt from these professional ups and downs. We have a unique opportunity to use our advanced training to help animals with disorders requiring complicated treatment. A properly chosen and performed operation can quickly alleviate pain and suffering and restore the pet's health and well-being. But invasive procedures carry risks, and even the most carefully performed surgery can result in complications, some of which may be life-threatening. A basic tenant of surgery is "Above all else, do no harm." Try as we may to follow that guideline, circumstances sometimes lead to a bad outcome, and some animal caregivers are quick to blame the surgeon for the morbidity or mortality associated with the procedure. The surgeon can experience joy from the successes but can be devastated by failure. Maintaining a steady demeanor through the ups and downs is difficult. Riding an emotional roller coaster can affect decision-making and judgment.

Some have asked how I manage to avoid these problems and stay mentally healthy. I think that some of the factors are inherent—an upbeat person by nature, I naturally focus on the positive and don't often struggle with toxic, destructive thinking. Other factors are lifestyle choices: I am physically active, preferring to spend time exercising and being outside where I can be in touch with nature. I have friends I can connect with, and most importantly, I have an emotionally intimate relationship with a few very close friends. These are people I trust to discuss my deepest feelings, sharing not just my successes, but my insecurities, frustrations, and failures. I know these friends will be by my side through life's journeys, no matter the trials and tribulations. The most important person is my wife, Becky. My energy, attitude, and emotional health are all fed by her love and devotion. Other family members, especially my children, Justin, Mary, and Stuart, are outlets for my affection. Thinking about them makes me feel good.

I have always felt that if your only source of self-esteem is your job, it can lead to a fragile existence. Finding balance in your life by having things you enjoy doing outside of work is essential, whether it's spirituality, meditation, hobbies, music, crafts, volunteer work, cooking, or other activities that give you a break from work stresses and strains. My favorite hobby is fly fishing, the sport of catching elusive and beautiful fish by casting tiny lures that look like insects. I put on my gear, wade out into a quiet, flowing river, tie on a tiny fly, and slowly cast it to the water. After a few minutes on the river, my mind transforms as I completely focus on the fishing —the rhythm of the cast, the water streaming between my legs, and the sound of the fish rising to the water's surface to sip the tiny bugs. The experience is quiet, relaxing, and meditative.

One thing I have recognized about myself is that I need validation. Whether due to my experience as a child or just an inner craving, I am constantly searching for attention from others. Fortunately, my academic career put me in a place where interaction with others came naturally. I love teaching and was able to immerse myself in educating veterinary students and being rewarded for it. The students and I fed off each other's positive energy—we had a mutually beneficial relationship which helped satisfy my appetite for feedback and encouragement.

Spending time with dogs and cats, whether as a doctor or owner, is also good for my soul. I try to share the animal's ability to focus on the present, to love unconditionally, to enjoy little moments of pleasure, and to forgive those who have hurt us. The animals I describe in this book, as well as the many who I have personally shared my life with, have taught me these most important lessons by example. They have helped me live a full and rewarding life, both professionally and personally, and I am grateful for all the animals who have enriched my world through our mutual love and companionship. With animals, we share what Abe Fortas called the "seamless web" of life, even when our lives are threatened by illness. I will always be in awe of a pet's ability not just to survive critical illness as in the stories told here, but their ability to make me feel like I am the most important thing in their life. We all need friendship, and who better to provide it than the warm, furry creature who right now at this late hour is lying at my feet keeping me company as I type these words?

Thank you for being with me, old friend. Tomorrow I promise to play ball with you.

References

1. Peacock E. E, & Van Winkle, W. (1970). *Surgery and Biology of Wound Repair.* WB Saunders.

2. Rader, R. (2018) Why You Should Stop Using Hydrogen Peroxide on Wounds. https://www.davisregional.com/news-room/why-you-should-stop-using-hydrogen-peroxide-on-wou-13469

3. Rankin, L. (2011). Can Positive Thinking Help You Heal? *Psychology Today*, December 27, 2011. https://www.psychologytoday.com/us/blog/owning-pink/201112/can-positive-thinking-help-you-heal

4. Faver, C. (2009). Seeking our place in the web of life: Animals and human spirituality. *Journal of Religion & Spirituality in Social Work: Social Thought. 28*(4), 362-378.

5. Selzer, R. (1981). *Mortal Lessons.* Chatto and Windus Ltd.

6. Bechert, K. & Abraham, S. (2009). Pain Management and Wound Care. *Journal of the American College of Certified Wound Specialists,* 1, 65–71.

7. Quain, A. & Khardori, N. (2015). Nutrition in wound care management: A comprehensive overview. *Wounds, 27*(12), 327-335.

8. Mphande, A., Killowe, C., Phalira, S., Jones, H. W., & Harrison, W. J. (2007). Effects of honey and

sugar dressings on wound healing. *Journal of Wound Care*, *16*(7), 317-9.

9. Reinhardt, V. & Reinhardt, A. The Magic of Touch. (2017). Animal Welfare Institute, 2nd ed. https://awionline.org/sites/default/files/publication/digital_download/AWI-LA-Magic-of-Touch.pdf

10. Corbee, R. & Van Kerkhoven, W. (2014) Nutritional support of dogs and cats after surgery or illness. *Open Journal of Veterinary Medicine*, 4, 44-57.

11. Winkler, K. Factors that interfere with wound healing. *Merck Veterinary Manual*. https://www.merckvetmanual.com/emergency-medicine-and-critical-care/wound-management/factors-that-interfere-with-wound-healing

12. Pavletic, M. M. (2010). Atlas of Small Animal Wound Management & Reconstructive surgery. 3rd ed. Wiley-Blackwell, Ames, 17-30, 81-126, 357-402, 511-534.

13. Strubel, A. (2018). Sunlight is the best medicine. Not a metaphor—science. *Center for Environmental Therapeutics*. https://cet.org/sunlight-is-the-best-medicine-not-a-metaphor-science/

14. Winch, G. 10 things you didn't know about guilt. https://www.psychologytoday.com/us/blog/the-squeaky-wheel/201411/10-things-you-didnt-know-about-guilt

15. Rovner, J. (2012). Pet therapy: How animals and humans heal each other. "Your Health," *NPR.*

https://www.npr.org/sections/health-shots/
2012/03/09/146583986/pet-therapy-how-animals-
and-humans-heal-each-other

16. Jarral, O., Jarral, R., Chan, K., & Punjabi, P. (2011). Use of a purse string suture in proximal coronary anastomosis to reduce size mismatch between conduit and aortotomy. *Annals of the Royal College of Surgeons of England*, *93*(5), 415–416.

17. Horowitz, A. (2009). *Inside of a Dog*. Scribner.

18. Sones, E., Smith, A., Schleis, S, Brawner, W., Almond, G., Taylor, K., Haney, S., Wypij, J., Keyerleber, M., Arthur, J., Hamilton, T., Lawrence, J., Gieger, T., Sellon, R., Wright, Z. (2013). Survival times for canine intranasal sarcomas treated with radiation therapy: 86 cases (1996-2011). *Vet Radiol Ultrasound*, *54*(2),194-201.

19. Soukup, J. W., Snyder, C. J., Gengler, W. R. (2009). Free auricular autograft for repair of an oronasal fistula in a dog. *J Vet Dent*, *26*(2), 86-95.

20. Cox, C. L., Hunt, G. B., Cadier, M. M. (2007). Repair of oronasal fistulae using auricular cartilage grafts in five cats. *Vet Surg*, 36, 164-169.

21. Jeschke, M. G., Pinto, R., Kraft, R., et.al. (2015). Morbidity and survival probability in burn patients in modern burn care. *Critical Care Medicine*, *43*(4), 808–815.

22. Wohlsein, P., Peters, M., Schulze, C., Baumgartner, W. (2016). Thermal injuries in veterinary forensic pathology. *Veterinary Pathology*, *53*(5), 1001-1017.

23. Simon, A.,[1] Traynor, K.,[2] Santos, K., et.al. (2009). Medical honey for wound care—Still the 'latest resort'? *Evidence-Based Complement Alternate Medicine, 6*(2), 165–173.

24. Rollin, B. E. (2009). An ethicist's commentary on multiple survival surgeries as a teaching method. Veterinary Medical Ethics, *Canadian Veterinary Journal*, 50, 901-904.

25. Gouin, J. & Kiecolt-Glaser, J. K. (2011). The impact of psychological stress on wound healing: Methods and mechanisms immunol. *Allergy Clin North Am., 31*(1), 81–93.

26. White, R.N., Burton, C. A. (2000). Surgical management of intrathoracic tracheal avulsion in cats: Long-term results in 9 consecutive cases. *Vet Surg, 29*(5), 430-435.

About the Authors

Dr. Stephen Birchard is a board-certified specialist in veterinary surgery and former professor of veterinary medicine at The Ohio State University College of Veterinary Medicine. He has published extensively in the clinical veterinary literature and is the chief editor or co-editor of several veterinary textbooks, including *The Saunders Manual of Small Animal Practice* (co-editor Robert Sherding). Dr. Birchard does online continuing education through his blog *Veterinary Key Points* and his educational Facebook page (*Dr. Stephen Birchard, Veterinary Continuing Education*). He shares his home with a menagerie of rescued pets including Calvin, a very talkative Labrador mix, Sofie, a food motivated beagle, and Creamsicle, a furry feline who excels at annoying the canines.

Co-author Mr. Fe Anam Avis is an experienced church consultant, author, and former pastor. His published works range from books addressing leadership transitions in churches to suicide prevention, including *Owl Sight: Evidence Based Discernment and the Promise of Organizational Intelligence for Ministry* and *A Second Day: A Hopeful Journey Out of Suicidal Thinking*.

Made in the USA
Monee, IL
05 April 2022